Cultural Studies of Rights

At a time of global uncertainties and erosion of liberties, how will cultural studies clear a space for a parallel intellectual and political engagement with human rights practice? How will human rights thinking be liberated from its doctrinal approach to ethics and legal justice?

Cultural Studies of Rights: Critical Articulations forges an alliance between cultural studies and human rights scholarships, to help us better understand the changing and complex political context that continuously shapes contemporary violence. To date, interdisciplinary dialogue or institutional collaboration remains rare across the two domains, resulting in critical interpretive work appearing too vacuous at times, and institutional legal work often trapped in doctrinalism. By opening a door for a new and engaging scholarship, this book will re-ignite debates and passions within communication and critical cultural studies in the search for global justice.

This book was originally published as a special issue of *Communication and Critical/Cultural Studies*.

John Nguyet Erni is Professor and Head of the Department of Cultural Studies at Lingnan University, Hong Kong. His books include *Internationalizing Cultural Studies: An Anthology* (2005, with Ackbar Abbas), *Asian Media Studies: The Politics of Subjectivities* (2005, with Siew Keng Chua), and *Unstable Frontiers: Technomedicine and the Cultural Politics of "Curing" AIDS* (1994). He has also published widely on critical public health, Chinese consumption of transnational culture, queer media, youth popular consumption in Hong Kong and Asia, and human rights politics. Besides his PhD, he has earned a Master of Laws specializing in human rights.

Cultural Studies of Rights
Critical Articulations

Edited by
John Nguyet Erni

LONDON AND NEW YORK

First published 2011
by Routledge

2 Park Square, Milton Park, Abingdon, Oxfordshire OX14 4RN
Simultaneously published in the USA and Canada
by Routledge
711 Third Avenue, New York, NY 10017

First issued in paperback 2014

Routledge is an imprint of the Taylor & Francis Group, an informa business

© 2012 National Communication Association

This book is a reproduction of *Communication and Critical/Cultural Studies*, Volume 7, Issue 3. The Publisher requests to those authors who may be citing this book to state, also, the bibliographical details of the special issue on which the book was based.

All rights reserved. No part of this book may be reprinted or reproduced or utilised in any form or by any electronic, mechanical, or other means, now known or hereafter invented, including photocopying and recording, or in any information storage or retrieval system, without permission in writing from the publishers.

Trademark notice: Product or corporate names may be trademarks or registered trademarks, and are used only for identification and explanation without intent to infringe.

British Library Cataloguing in Publication Data
A catalogue record for this book is available from the British Library

ISBN 13: 978-0-415-67729-5 (hbk)
ISBN 13: 978-1-138-00895-3 (pbk)

DOI: 10.4324/9781315872636

Disclaimer
The publisher would like to make readers aware that the chapters in this book are referred to as articles as they had been in the special issue. The publisher accepts responsibility for any inconsistencies that may have arisen in the course of preparing this volume for print.

Contents

Notes on Contributors vi
Acknowledgements vii

1. Reframing Cultural Studies: Human Rights as a Site of Legal-cultural Struggles
   John Nguyet Erni 1

2. Honing a Critical Cultural Study of Human Rights
   Rosemary J. Coombe 10

3. Immanent Law and the Juridical: Toward a Liberative Ontology of Human Rights
   Hans Skott-Myhre & Donato Tarulli 27

4. Human Rights and an Ethic of truths: Pragmatic Dilemmas and Discursive Interventions
   Leonard C. Hawes 41

5. Exiled Writers, Human Rights, and Social Advocacy Movements in Australia: A Critical Fugal Analysis
   Ruth Skilbeck 60

6. The Abuses of Literacy: Amazon Kindle and the Right to Read
   Ted Striphas 77

7. The Postcolonial Predicament of Gay Rights in the *Queen Boat* Affair
   Julian Awwad 98

Index 117

Notes on Contributors

Julian Awwad is an Assistant Professor in the Department of Communication Studies at Concordia University in Montreal, Canada. He holds a PhD in Communication Studies from the Department of Art History and Communication Studies, McGill University. His teaching and research interests include postcolonial theory and criticism, global communication, media and cultural globalization, intersections of law, communication, and culture, and Arab media, culture, and society.

Rosemary J. Coombe is Senior Canada Research Chair in Law, Communication and Culture at York University, Canada.

John Nguyet Erni is Professor and Head of the Department of Cultural Studies at Lingnan University, Hong Kong. His books include *Internationalizing Cultural Studies: An Anthology* (2005, with Ackbar Abbas), *Asian Media Studies: The Politics of Subjectivities* (2005, with Siew Keng Chua), and *Unstable Frontiers: Technomedicine and the Cultural Politics of "Curing" AIDS* (1994). He has also published widely on critical public health, Chinese consumption of transnational culture, queer media, youth popular consumption in Hong Kong and Asia, and human rights politics. Besides his PhD, he has earned a Master of Laws specializing in human rights.

Leonard C. Hawes is Professor of Communication at the University of Utah, USA, where he teaches courses in cultural studies, critical theory, communication theory, and conflict studies. He is the co-founder of the Graduate Conflict Resolution Certificate Program at the University of Utah. Currently, he is completing a book, *Desiring Utterances: Process, Conflict, Discourse*, based on his experience working with cultural conflicts in Denmark and the United States.

Ruth Skilbeck researches and lectures in Communication at the University of Technology, Sydney, Australia.

Hans Skott-Myhre is an Associate Professor in the Department of Child and Youth Studies at Brock University, Canada.

Ted Striphas is Associate Professor in the Department of Communication and Culture, Indiana University, USA. He is author of *The Late Age of Print: Everyday Book Culture from Consumerism to Control* (2009).

Donato Tarulli is an Associate Professor in the Department of Child and Youth Studies at Brock University, Canada.

Acknowledgements

John Nguyet Erni would like to thank Lingnan University, Hong Kong, for a Direct Research Grant that helped support this project.

Rosemary Coombe would like to thank the Stellenbosch Institute for Advanced Study for its support for her writing project, and Nicole Aylwin, Lisa Norton, and Andrew Jacob for research and editorial assistance.

Hans Skott-Myhre and Donato Tarulli thank John Nguyet Erni, Greg Wise, and an anonymous reviewer for their assistance and helpful suggestions for revision.

The research project discussed in Ruth Skilbeck's essay was assisted by a grant from the Australian Centre for Independent Journalism, at the University of Technology, Sydney.

Ted Striphas wishes to thank Phaedra C. Pezzullo, John Nguyet Erni, the anonymous CCCS reviewers, and the wise crowd at the Differences and Repetitions wiki (http://striphas.wikidot.com/acknowledged-goods-worksite) for helpful feedback on this essay.

Reframing Cultural Studies: Human Rights as a Site of Legal-cultural Struggles[1]

John Nguyet Erni

In the twenty-first century, after more than 60 years of development since its rise to prominence worldwide, the modern human rights system has become a common, even popular, public and policy discourse. It has also generated a complicated matrix of legal institutions, doctrines, litigation practices, and social movements. Across the popular and legal domains, human rights have been a persistent object of analysis by well-recognized social scientists and thinkers, such as Bryan Turner, Will Kymlicka, Armatya Sen, Boaventura de Sousa Santos, Martha Nussbaum, Jurgen Habermas, Janet Halley, Patricia Williams, Jack Donnelly, Malcolm Waters, and many others. Using institutional, discourse, and critical approaches, the human rights enterprise has been critiqued by sociologists,[2] political scientists,[3] anthropologists,[4] international relations scholars,[5] and of course many legal scholars. Yet before the 1970s, almost all academic work on human rights was provided by legal scholars and lawyers, with most work appearing in law journals. Meanwhile, through the 1970s and 1980s, surveys on the teaching of human rights in universities found an overwhelming dominance of the legal perspective.[6]

The intervention of critical cultural theory into human rights theories and debates has been relatively rare. Balakrishnan Rajagopal is among a few who offer a detailed examination of the encounter between a new sensibility to reconstruct international law by legal practitioners in post-World War II times and the emergence of a new discourse of development-based social movement aimed at addressing issues of growth and poverty in the Global South.[7] Another important figure is Boaventura de Sousa Santos, whose analysis, among other things, of the World Social Forum (WSF)—a broad global rights-based movement—utilizes left thinking linked to Latin American cultural theories, so as to rethink the organizational changes in the WSF to address global social justice concerns.[8]

More broadly, there have also been some analyses of power, hegemony, and even neoliberalism in human rights practices by a small number of socio-legal theorists and comparativists from the United States and Europe, along with several constitutional scholars from non-Western countries.[9] Socio-legal analyses have explicitly relied on prominent cultural theorists, such as Foucault,[10] Gramsci,[11] Fanon,[12] Butler,[13] to name only a few. As well, there have been critical studies of the United Nations and its associated policies, e.g., from an institutional perspective,[14] a feminist point of view,[15] and a postcolonial perspective.[16]

It goes without saying that cultural studies and human rights practices have different genealogies. Whereas the former is grounded in anti-foundational philosophy, critical sociology, critical theory in the humanities, and interpretive social sciences, the latter is deeply influenced by Kantian philosophy, natural law, positive law traditions, and social movement literature. While there are philosophical incompatibilities between them, there are also intellectual and political synergies. To date, however, intellectual dialogue or interdisciplinary/institutional collaboration remain very rare across the divide.

I came into contact with human rights debates through an interdisciplinary program at Columbia University. In 1999, I held a Rockefeller Fellowship that enabled me to participate in the then newly established Program on Gender, Sexuality, Health, and Human Rights.[17] The Program was an intellectual enterprise established by Carol Vance to engage with the multiple forms of social, political, cultural, and postcolonial wars against non-normative genders and sexualities. This enterprise culminated in the weekly seminars, which saw participation from feminists, representatives of community groups, critical-minded staff and graduate students, and human rights advocates, analysts, and practitioners. While very few of those participants directly allied themselves with cultural studies *per se*, the discussion in the weekly seminars intersected tacitly with it by means of a shared critical sensibility, a more or less common academic vocabulary drawn from a broad Marxist, feminist, subalternist, and postmodernist ethos, and finally, a crypto-critique of the relevance of cultural studies itself. As our discussion began to take shape around a complicated set of concerns brought about by theories of gender and sexuality, the various forms of public health practices that contoured international body politics, and the community based activist-oriented critique, the discussion was also frequently dominated by a human rights legal perspective. A rights-based discourse in formal legalistic terms as well as in the more informal terms of oppositional critique of law, was not only leading our discussion, it effectively colonized it. I mention earlier the presence of a crypto-critique of the relevance of cultural studies. The inadequacy of cultural studies in using its analytical tools to speak about the problematics at hand became a tacitly agreed-upon fact among the participants. The "shame," if you will, was subtly cast in the form of cultural studies' lack of institutional knowledge of, or strategic political capital in, either rights-based discourse or legal-based intervention. The tacit or hidden agreement about the seeming irrelevance of cultural studies, while not manifesting in any direct attack on cultural studies, nevertheless silenced it. To me, the experience was one of intellectual reinvigoration via a strange form of (self-)silencing. I found myself troubled by a certain kind of theoretical as well as political reductionism in an intellectual atmosphere dominated by human rights discourse and international law.[18] In this particular context, are human rights discourses and international law those that one cannot not want?

Mostly I remember feeling very uneasy with a certain kind of self-assurance of political certainty. I felt that human rights were too easily taken as a rallying point to either express various modes of injury, or to attack various forms of nationalism that inflict those injuries. Yet at the same time, I was immensely seduced by the rights discourse and international law. I felt that those were clearly blindspots in cultural studies' whole theoretical apparatus for thinking through questions of power and politics. That a complicated engagement through an oscillation between skepticism and seduction was conducted via (self-)silencing, convinced me that cultural studies somehow must render itself more "relevant" without sacrificing its anti-reductionist stance.[19] Facing the problem of cultural studies' apparent lack of relevance, we may be compelled to ask what is *after* cultural studies as we know it today, by abandoning those elements of the field that lead to mere self-reproduction, thus relinquishing a certain barrier to other critical impulses.

Is There a Legal Cultural Studies?

Generally speaking, cultural studies holds a profoundly skeptical view of law, probably because of the latter's imbrications in power, forms of knowledge, systems of disciplining social subjects and groups, and modes of modern surveillance and governance. But a cultural analysis/cultural studies of law not only can help to challenge static ideas of culture, it may also help to advance new conceptions of law. For instance, Andrew Ross posits a new model of cultural studies analysis of multicultural legal relations in the United States. At the center of his analysis is the "politics of recognition in law" that can help reshape what he calls "cultural justice" of cultural minorities.[20] Toby Miller, on the other hand, calls for legal engagement within cultural studies to demonstrate the latter's utility in addressing labor dispute issues.[21] In addressing the issue of torture, Allen Feldman has turned to visual theories to unpack the discursive understanding of the events of Abu Ghraib prison in international news.[22] On Abu Ghraib, Henry Giroux has also advanced his analysis of the pedagogical potential of the shocking photographs of torture and the political regime behind the torture policies.[23] In these and other works, many of the methods used by cultural studies, including deconstruction, genealogy, psychoanalysis, Marxist dialectics, and feminism are adopted, thereby forging an understanding of human rights as a site of legal-cultural struggles.

The collection of original essays for this special issue, in my mind, helps to open a door for realizing a symbiotic convergence between human rights practices and cultural studies. They attempt to bring about that particular articulation in order to understand better the changing and complex political context that continuously shapes contemporary ethical debates. They focus on the way in which we may reconceive human rights—including the epistemologies, assumptions, relations, practices, and institutions of the rights discourse as they are imagined politically and legally—in order to remap the ethico-political commitments of cultural studies from *within* a "rights imaginary."

Rosemary Coombe's specially commissioned essay for this collection is built from her long-standing work that endeavors to bridge the methods and theories in anthropology, law, and cultural studies.[24] Her essay carefully deciphers the epistemological contradictions between human rights and cultural studies, and attempts to overcome them. Taking the complexity of the concept of culture to heart, Coombe laments that "culture" is, ironically, often that which mires critics in unfortunate dichotomies, such as those of universalism/relativism, and thus fails to advance critical reflexivity around issues of rights and culture. Meanwhile, to her, it is patently clear that "[t]o the extent that issues of social exclusion, inequality, identity, power and representation engage us, cultural studies are *practically* invested in human rights discourse and praxis." Coombe's critical survey of legal theory and the humanities in her essay extends an opening to cultural studies scholars, despite the fact that "one of the more disconcerting revelations of reading across culturally-oriented human rights scholarship is how far from dialogic it is." In the end, Coombe suggests that the most productive site of articulation lies in legal and cultural anthropology, in which ethnographic study of the social and political meaning and consequence of rights-based practices in cultural and historical contexts dovetails with George Yudice's idea of "culture as resource." Coombe's strategic articulation here is one of the rare successes I have seen in opening a door for a future critical cultural study of human rights.

Leonard Hawes's essay, as well as Hans Skott-Myhre and Donato Tarulli's collaborative essay, approach the whole question about the symbiotic convergence of human rights and cultural studies from an ontological ground, while bearing in mind the complex political expressions that such an ontology of human rights can enable. Both essays are deeply influenced by a certain strand of cultural studies that radically questions the ontological stability of any concept. In this way, the very concept of "rights"—either as abstract universalist moralism or state-governed and politically negotiated moralism—is profoundly suspect. In Hawes's essay, he draws on Michael Ignatieff's position about human rights that argues how the invocation of rights often fixes social positions, abstracts those positions from lived experience, and moralizes rights in ways that render them inviolable, thus "leaving open only the options of righteous litigation and pietistic war." Hawes reminds us of the fundamental indeterminacy of rights, which is also a corollary of the inherent instability of rights: "Rights do not and cannot exist in isolation. Each rights-based claim fits into a background of other rights-based claims that can be used to define the limits of any particular right drawn into any particular controversy." Dissatisfied with a general tendency even among critical human rights work to reify rights and the subjects seeking them, Hawes turns to Alain Badiou to enable him to reformulate the human rights discourse. "For Badiou, truths of partisan, singular and unique universality … hold to the possibility of the emergence of the Same-which-is-not-yet. It is the 'which-is-not-yet' portion of that phrase that is important to understand," write Hawes. To deny this imminence, especially in the context of human rights advocacy, is to amount to what Badiou calls "Evil." Working with the imminent, on the other hand, allows one to see the complexity of different scales and planes of the experience of violence and injury. It is here that Hawes brings his conflict resolution work in Denmark to bear on the question of "rights-which-are-not-yet," as it were. He describes his work as alternative interventions to address "the escalating intensities of affect and libidinal conflicts" among different groups of Danish nationals and immigrants facing challenges to assert their rights. In the end, Hawes's reframing of the ontological crisis of the conventional human rights discourse pushes him to enact what he calls a "post-humanist communication ethic of truths."

Like Hawes, Skott-Myhre and Tarulli write from a position of skepticism toward the modernist ontology of human rights that ensnares the social subject of rights within the control of the sovereign state and its laws. Keeping close to law, as opposed to some vague expression of rights, Skott-Myhre and Tarulli work through Kafka's famous parable, "Before the Law," to suggest how the subject in front of the law is reduced to a "supplicant" who "entreats and expends in hopes of obtaining his desired end, while the mediating force [of law] defers and denies." Their contention in the essay is that sovereignty law and its "logic of the machinery of transcendent control" is in contestation with the liberative creative capacity of the subject, a "radically idiosyncratic subject of infinite creative autopoiesis," which they refer to as the "multitude." In this way, Skott-Myhre and Tarulli turn from Foucault to Spinoza and Derrida, in search of a non-juridical forms of law and of the subject produced within the philosophical landscape of immanence. Their project therefore reframes human rights not as a form of juridical petition to the sovereign state and its (modernist) laws for the permission to act, but instead as immanent potentialities.

What Coombe, Hawes, and Skott-Myhre and Tarulli have in common are the ways in which they destabilize *both* human rights and cultural studies as conceptual borders and as critical practices. In the essays by Ted Striphas, Ruth Skilbeck, and Julian Awwad, we are presented with three case studies that similarly challenge the notions of culture, rights, law, politics, and governmentality. The specific grounds of the rights of reading (Striphas), writing (Skilbeck) and the sexual self (Awwad) are pitched neither through abstracted empiricism nor grand moralism in the service of critique. Rather, the authors attend to networks, governmentalist technologies, texts, and the distributional concerns of the cultural economy so as to examine the specific modes of rights-inflected, and not necessarily rights-grounded, subject formation.

Striphas's essay takes Amazon's Kindle as what he calls an "illiberal" object, whose insertion into everyday life impedes, rather than enhances, the right of reading and literacy more generally. Kindle, which Striphas correctly argues as a strange commodity that attempts to simulate *and* exceed the book simultaneously, emerged out of the corporate transformation of Amazon from being a mere seller of books to a vast computing and data-mining infrastructure. Striphas's analysis shows us that reading on the Kindle amounts to a type of "reading labor" for the capture of surplus value by Amazon through its data-mining capability. Amazon extracts the electronic trails of one's reading choices on the Kindle for data aggregation purposes that turn a profit. Equally problematic, Striphas argues, is the fact that this surplus value is extracted through a practice that is akin to surveillance. While disciplinary surveillance does trouble Striphas, he also wants to attend to a much more subtle form of intrusion taking place at the level of everyday "sovereignty" and "solitude" of the reader: "Kindle ... runs afoul of the liberal belief in the sanctity of reading and hence the impulse to safeguard the sovereignty of readers." To Striphas, "liberal propriety" must be rigorously defended because, as he hints in his essay, literacy in the current technocultural commercial environment has been seriously threatened. This is not because access or the right to information is in anyway obstructed, but because the exuberance of the informational space, of which Kindle and other similar electronic devices are a part, has jeopardized the cultural space of, and the right to, reading conceived of as a practice of liberal virtue.

Creativity and politics, or rather creativity-in-politics, form the locus in Ruth Skilbeck's essay that looks at how the practice of writing intervenes in human rights cases. Cultural and political creativity, in the specific form of what Skilbeck calls "fugal writing," is not only a non-representational theoretical practice hailed via Kristeva, Bhabha, and Bahktin, but also a form of life-saving writing practice that restores the rights of survival and dignity. Her essay centers on the plight of two exiled writers—an Iranian poet and a journalist from the Ivory Coast—and their stories of arbitrary detention in Australia. Skilbeck argues that dialogic, polyphonic communication between the exiled writers and their advocates provides a "modal" shift from reading *about* to one of active writing *of*. This modal shift produces, among other things, a shift from the term "exiled writers" used merely as a metaphor, to a phenomenological-based analysis of actual cases of exiled writers. Phenomenological experience, according to Skilbeck, impacts upon the researcher and causes profound reflexive affects, motivating a deeper level of engagement.

Finally, Julian Awaad's essay on the case of gay rights as profoundly imbricated in the Egyptian state's maneuvering of postcolonial, nationalist, and religious sentiments, as well as legal protocols, illustrates how the cultural studies of minoritarian subjectivity can fruitfully intersect with a rights-based critique. The "Queen Boat 52" case of 2001 remains the most highly-publicized crackdown on same-sex practices in an Arab country. Awaad's project is to consider the conundrum of human rights work in intervening in the case when "rights-as-method," as it were, might restore a Western universalizing discourse and thus might risk being appropriated by the Egyptian state, as well as Arab intellectuals, in mounting an orientalist attack of human rights work, and at the same time, when "rights-as-disavowal" might leave state violence to go unaccounted for and unchallenged. Awaad's formulation or response to this conundrum is to reframe human rights as a productive paradox: "Egypt's postcolonial condition, like that of other Arab countries, necessitates a human rights framework which is based on a discourse and strategies for attaining sexual rights that activists *cannot not* want to employ, thereby legitimizing human rights work as a practical *strategy* informed by postcolonial perspectives." Consequently, the Queen Boat incident enables a critical reflection of the state of "gay subjectivity" as not always already subaltern, yet always a strategically available category for postcolonial rearticulation.

Existing cultural studies of law tends to rely too much on the predication of "agency" as a function of social and political imaginary structures. That is to say, it posits social consciousness and relations as always already historical and/or linguistic and/or symbolic. This important insight in cultural studies, however, does not sufficiently link "agency" with concrete institutions and institutional conduct shaped by the power relations inhered within institutions. The turn to the anthropology of cultural rights, to social movements and the institutional apparatus of law, as suggested by the essays in this collection, presents a remedy or at least an added layer in cultural studies' encounter with human rights. Cultural studies has long been attentive to the complex interpenetrations of power, agency, and the social imaginary. The field can indeed have a lot to say about how the rights-based meanings and actions are constituted by a variety of institutions, structures, and practices that comprise culture, and that those institutions, structures, and practices are themselves encapsulated, though always incompletely, in legal forms, regulations, and symbols. Thus, reading law and culture together as inter-implicated entities is a complex interpretive task. This collection, and the larger project of legal-cultural articulation behind it, attempts to open up such a door for a new and engaging kind of scholarship to flow.

Notes

[1] This project has benefited from financial support from the Research and Postgraduate Studies Committee of Lingnan University, Hong Kong Special Administrative Region, China (Project #: DR09B2).

[2] See B.S. Turner, "Introduction: Rights and Communities: Prolegomenon to a Sociology of Rights," *Australian and New Zealand Journal of Sociology* 31 (1995): 1–8; M. Waters, "Human Rights and the Universalization of Interests: Towards a Social Constructionist Approach," *Sociology* 30 (1996): 593–600; A. Woodiwiss, *Globalization, Human Rights and Labour Law in Pacific Asia* (Cambridge: Cambridge University Press, 1998).

[3] R.P. Claude and B.H. Weston, "International Human Rights: Overviews," in *Human Rights in the World Community: Issues and Action*, 2nd ed., ed. R.P. Claude and B.H. Weston, (Philadelphia, PA: University of Pennsylvania Press, 1992), 1–14; J. Foweraker and T. Landman, *Citizenship Rights and Social Movements* (Oxford: Oxford University Press, 1997); W. Kymlicka, "Human Rights and Ethnocultural Justice," in *Politics in the Vernacular: Nationalism, Multiculturalism and Citizenship*, ed. W. Kymlicka (Oxford: Oxford University Press, 2001), 69–90; J. McCamant, "Social Science and Human Rights," *International Organizations* 35 (1981): 531–52.

[4] T.E. Downing, "Human Rights Research: The Challenge for Anthropologists," in *Human Rights and Antropology*, ed. T.E. Downing and G. Kushner (Cambridge, MA: Cultural Survival, 1988): 9–19; J. Schirmer, "Universal and Sustainable Human Rights: Special Tribunals in Guatemala," in *Human Rights, Culture and Context: Anthropological Perspectives*, ed. R.A. Wilson (London: Pluto Press, 1997), 161–86.

[5] J. Donnelly, "The Social Construction of International Human Rights," in *Human Rights in Global Politics*, ed. T. Dunne and N.J. Wheeler (Cambridge: Cambridge University Press,

1999), 71–102; R.J. Vincent, *Human Rights and International Relations*. (Cambridge: Cambridge University Press, 1986).

[6] M. Freeman, *Human Rights: An Interdisciplinary Approach* (Cambridge: Polity Press): 77–8.

[7] Balakrishnan Rajagopal, "From Resistance to Renewal: The Third World, Social Movements, and the Expansion of International Institutions," *Harvard International Law Journal* 41, (2000): 529–78; Balakrishnan Rajagopal, "International Law and Social Movements: Challenges of Theorizing Resistance," *Columbia Journal of Transnational Law* 41 (2003): 397–433.

[8] Boaventura de Sousa Santos, "Beyond Neoliberal Governance: The World Social Forum as Subaltern Cosmopolitan Politics and Legality," in *Law and Globalization from Below: Towards a Cosmopolitan Legality*, ed. Boaventura de Sousa Santos and César Rodríguez-Garavito (Cambridge: Cambridge University Press, 2005); Boaventura de Sousa Santos, "Human Rights as an Emancipatory Script? Cultural and Political Conditions," in *Another Knowledge is Possible: Beyond Northern Epistemologies*, ed. Boaventura de Sousa Santos (London: Verso, 2007); Boaventura de Sousa Santos, "The World Social Forum and the Global Left," *Politics & Society* 36 (2008): 247–70.

[9] Upendra Baxi, "Universal Rights and Cultural Pluralism: Constitutionalism as a Site of State Formative Practices," *Cardoza Law Review* 21 (2000): 1183–210; J.N. Erni, "New Sovereignties and Neoliberal Ethics: Remapping the Human Rights Imaginary," *Cultural Studies* 23 (2009): 417–36; David Kairys, *The Politics of Law: A Progressive Critique*, 3rd. ed. (New York: Basic Books, 1998); Julie Mertus, "From Legal Transplants to Transformative Justice: Human Rights and the Promise of Transnational Civil Society," *American University International Law Review* 14 (1999): 1335–89; Austin Sarat, *The Blackwell Companion to Law and Society* (Malden, MA: Blackwell Publishing, 2004).

[10] See Tawia Ansah, "A Terrible Purity: International Law, Morality, Religion, Exclusion," *Cornell International Law Journal* 38 (2005): 9–70; Larry Cata Backer, "Reifying Law—Government, Law and the Rule of Law in Governance Systems," *Penn State International Law Review* 26 (2008): 511–20; Pheng Cheah, *Inhuman Conditions: On Cosmopolitanism and Human Rights* (Cambridge, MA: Harvard University Press, 2004; Brent Pickett, "Foucaultian rights?," *The Social Science Journal* 37 (2000): 403–21.

[11] Andrew Levin, "Civil Society and Democratization in Haiti," *Emory International Law Review* 9 (1995): 389–457; Anthony Taibi, "Racial Justice in the Age of the Global Economy: Community Empowerment and Global Strategy," *Duke Law Journal* 44 (1995): 928–84; Ugo Mattei and Jeffrey Lena, "U.S. Jurisdiction Over Conflicts Arising Outside of the United States: Some Hegemonic Implications," *Hastings International & Comparative Law Review* 24 (2001): 381–400.

[12] See Jeffrey Brown, "Beyond Nationalism and Toward a Dynamic Theory of Pan-African Unity," *Berkeley Journal of African-American Law & Policy* 8 (2006): 60–78.

[13] See Johanna Bond, "International Intersectionality: A Theoretical and Pragmatic Exploration of Women's International Human Rights Violations," *Emory Law Journal* 52 (2003): 71–85; Sami Zeidan, "The Limits of Queer Theory in LGBT Litigation and the International Human Rights Discourse," *Willamette Journal of International Law & Dispute Resolution* 14 (2006): 73–96.

[14] See Richard Glick, "Lip Service to the Laws of War: Humanitarian Law and United Nations Armed Forces," *Michigan Journal of International Law* 17 (1995): 53–107; Felicia Swindells, "UN Sanctions in Haiti: A Contradiction Under Articles 41 and 55 of the UN Charter," *Fordham International Law Journal* 20 (1997): 1880–960.

[15] See Hilary Charlesworth, "Not Waving but Drowning: Gender Mainstreaming and Human Rights in the United Nations," *The Harvard Human Rights Journal* 18 (2005): 1–17; Karen Engle, "'Calling in the Troops': The Uneasy Relationship Among Women's Rights, Human Rights, and Humanitarian Intervention," *Harvard Human Rights Journal* 20 (2007): 189–226.

[16] See Karin Mickelson, "Rhetoric and Rage: Third World Voices in International Legal Discourse," *Wisconsin International Law Journal* 16 (1998): 353–419; Benjamin Richardson, "Environmental Law in Postcolonial Societies: Straddling the Local–Global Institutional Spectrum," *Colorado Journal of International Environmental Law and Policy* 11 (2000); 1–82.

[17] See http://www.cumc.columbia.edu/dept/gender/

[18] I told this story in John N. Erni, "Who Needs Human Rights: Cultural Studies and Public Institutions," in *Instituting Cultural Studies*, ed. Meaghan Morris and Mette Hjort, (Hong Kong: Hong Kong University Press, forthcoming).

[19] In 2005, the author completed a Master of Laws studies specializing in Human Rights at the University of Hong Kong.

[20] Andrew Ross, "Components of Cultural Justice," in *The Fate of Law*, ed. Austin Sarat and Thomas Kearns (Ann Arbor, MI: University of Michigan Press, 1991), 203–28.

[21] Toby Miller, "What It Is and what It Isn't: Cultural Studies Meets Graduate-Student Labor," *Yale Journal of Law and Humanities* 13 (2001): 69–94.

[22] Allen Feldman, "On the Actuarial Gaze: From 9/11 to Abu Ghraib," *Cultural Studies* 19 (2005): 203–26.

[23] Henry Giroux, *Against the New Authoritarianism: Politics after Abu Ghraib* (Winnipeg, Manitoba: Abeiter Ring Publishing, 2005).

[24] See, e.g., Rosemary Coombe, *The Cultural Life of Intellectual Properties: Authorship, Appropriation and the Law* (Durham, NC: Duke University Press, 1998); Rosemary Coombe, "Legal Claims to Culture in and Against the Market: Neoliberalism and the Global Proliferation of Meaningful Difference," *Law, Culture and the Humanities* 1 (2005): 32–55; Rosemary Coombe, "The Expanding Purview of Cultural Properties and their Politics," *Annual Review of Law and Social Sciences* 5 (2009): 393–412.

Honing a Critical Cultural Study of Human Rights

Rosemary J. Coombe

A critical cultural studies of human rights has yet to emerge as an interdisciplinary field of study. Despite the proliferation of scholarly work in legal philosophy and law and humanities over the past decade, we have seen little by way of sustained dialogue between critics of rights or conversations between rights critics and theorists of culture. Nonetheless, the characteristic approaches, concerns, concepts, and methods of cultural studies are both appropriate and necessary in a global policy environment that has put increasing emphasis upon cultural identity and cultural resources in both rights-based practices and neoliberal governmentalities, suggesting new avenues of inquiry.

A critical cultural study of human rights is nascent, rather than emergent. There are numerous studies of international human rights as a dominant discourse and practice informed by many varieties of critical social theory, but those who adopt the perspectives, methods, and concepts characteristic of cultural studies do not yet form a community of interlocutors engaged in a shared critical project. This is not surprising because it is daunting task. Such an endeavor requires a capacity to read across many fields of specialized expertise in law, philosophy, and politics—while being captured by none of them. If this project were to mirror the richness of critical cultural studies more generally, it might ideally combine the strengths of a rigorous political economy perspective with the interpretive tools of rhetoric, hermeneutics, semiotics, discourse theory, deconstructionism, science and technology studies, and psychoanalytic inquiry (readers will no doubt have other ingredients to add to this mix). We might also adopt an analysis sensitive to issues of discipline, subject formation and governmentality, informed by theories of practice, generated through and animated by ethnographic research. Such an ideal is a long way from being realized, but there are many promising efforts on which to build.

Culture in Human Rights and the Cultural Studies of Human Rights

We might expect to find that of all of the various subfields of human rights, cultural studies would have a particular interest in the field of cultural rights. According to the major international covenants, these include rights to the moral and material interests in works of which one is an author (which include but are not limited to intellectual property protections); rights to participate in community cultural life; rights to enjoy the arts and share in scientific advancement and its benefits (often glossed in terms of technology); and state encouragement of international contacts and cooperation. Nonetheless, the scholarship exploring this subfield of law—historically, doctrinally, philosophically, or empirically—is pitifully small. Cultural rights have attracted remarkably little critical theoretical attention. This task may be especially challenging because the individual rights pertaining to culture delineated above are augmented by collective rights to cultural integrity, cultural heritage rights, and rights of indigenous peoples premised on cultural grounds. Recent UNESCO Conventions have put new emphasis upon intangible cultural heritage, cultural diversity, and intercultural dialogue, further populating this field of law and the activities generated in its name.

Indeed, the practice of cultural studies shares with the practice of human rights constitutive conflicts over the meaning of the culture concept fundamental to this universalizing, if never universal, field of endeavour that simultaneously constitutes an institutionalized political economy and a nascent, aspirational politics. Human rights law allows culture to be both subject to and the subject of rights claims in contradictory ways.[1] When professing the rights of individuals to express, enjoy, and have access to culture, modern aesthetic ideals are indexed while other cultural rights, such as those traditionally articulated by state parties to UNESCO conventions, often resemble affirmations of Herderian Romantic nationalism. Subnational and transnational cultural rights have only slowly gained acceptance in international rights fora where anthropological approaches to culture as a way of life coexist with emerging understandings of culture as a popular, expressive, world-making activity. More recently, the enhanced value placed on cultural diversity and protections for minority peoples has encouraged the articulation of an ever greater range of collective rights, expressed culturally, which are used to ground claims for land, education, and environmental protection as well as for new forms of autonomy considered as means of cultural survival.[2] Culture may be used to support progressive as well as reactionary claims, legitimating environmental struggles against predatory modern extractive developments, and anti-globalization movements as well as celebrating old antagonisms and entrenched privileges.[3] Unfortunately, the conflictual meanings of the culture concept in human rights discourse has tended to mire critics in unfortunate dichotomies, such as those of universalism/relativism, that have forestalled rather than advanced critical reflexivity around issues of rights and culture.

Many of the subfields of cultural rights have been areas of cultural studies concern. The cultural and communicative impact of the growing expansion of intellectual property rights, equity issues with respect to access to information and technology, and the relationship between communications and development are obvious examples. Practitioners of cultural studies have pioneered research on cultural identity, multiculturalism and cosmopolitanism, and the inclusions and exclusions characteristic of the dominant cultural texts and practices of social communities and their imaginaries. We have seen a growth of important studies addressing cultural work, cultural economies, cultural exchange, cultural commodification, and critical evaluation of emergent discourses and practices of creative and cultural industries. We might consider all of these as properly issues of cultural policy,[4] an area of cultural studies appropriately subject to renewed critical scrutiny[5] given new strategies of capital accumulation based on informational capital. These broad-ranging studies have not, however, considered these as interlinked issues within a legal or theoretical field of cultural rights, nor have they normatively deployed a discourse of rights in arguing for social change. Nonetheless, there are grounds for heeding Bennett and Mercer's[6] call to deepen the tools of cultural policy research and analysis by delineating the contours of an emerging legal, institutional, and political terrain in which cultural rights and cultural claims assume new political and economic significance in an increasingly transnational field of cultural policy.[7]

The significance of human rights to cultural studies is, in any case, by no means exhausted by cultural rights, however inadequately the latter have been addressed, and however much one might hope that cultural studies could influence policy by better attending to these as an integrated group of issues. Rather than enumerate categories and types of human rights and scholarly work that consider them to some degree, I will suggest that the very ways in which cultural studies has generally distinguished its topics, perspectives, and approaches suggests particular vantage points and portals into the human rights terrain. For example, we might revisit Richard Johnson's classic essay, "What is Cultural Studies, Anyway?"[8] and propose that cultural studies consider human rights texts in a wide field of contexts including their production and reproduction, interpretive consumption or reception, and circulation within socially and symbolically differentiated fields of practice. The relationship between "the word and the world"[9] in human rights projects is especially daunting because human rights are textual expressions that ideally set out to encompass and abstract principles sufficient to human flourishing. Although this omniscient positioning makes human rights rhetoric an easy target for anti-canonical scholars inclined to undermine meta-theory, the evidently elastic capacity of human rights to encompass and embrace ever greater fields of human difference in a global project of enhancing human dignity, makes most criticism—of their false universalism and actual particularism, their Eurocentrism, androcentrism, heterosexism and degree of inclusivity, for example—a contribution to the practice of human rights, rather than an indictment of it. To the extent that issues of social exclusion, inequality, identity, power, and representation engage us, cultural studies are *practically* invested in human rights discourse and praxis.

Theoretical work on human rights has proliferated dramatically in the last decade, particularly in the wake of political transformations set in motion by 9/11. First introducing key dimensions of human rights as law, politics, ideology, and governmentality, I will reference work in legal theory and the humanities that adopts approaches with which cultural studies scholars are familiar and takes perspectives with which they are likely to be sympathetic. It is difficult to summarize even this limited range of scholarship given the utter lack of synthetic work accomplished by these scholars to date; one of the more disconcerting revelations of reading across culturally oriented human rights scholarship is how far from dialogic it is. The lack of cross-referencing and critical consideration of contemporaneous arguments (even among scholars who share similar philosophical positions) suggests that even within the closely-related fields of law, literature and rhetoric, nothing approaching a critical cultural studies of human rights is emerging. This survey is not exhaustive; I have chosen representative examples of approaches and positions that seem most relevant to the interests and proclivities of cultural studies scholars. Others no doubt could be chosen.

I will then suggest that some of the scholarship that might best contribute to a critical cultural study of human rights is offered by legal and cultural anthropologists. Although notoriously shy about articulating general theoretical principles,[10] they offer frameworks influenced by continental social and critical theory for the study of rights derived from the ethnographic study of the social and political meaning and consequence of rights-based practices in cultural and historical contexts. I conclude by exploring how a fuller elaboration of George Yudice's[11] concept of culture as a resource in strategies of public action[12] provides promising avenues for the future critical cultural study of human rights.

Human Rights as Ideology, Discourse, and Neoliberal Hegemony

Human rights nominate a field of law and politics that has its conceptual origins in Western political philosophy and statecraft. It frames a field of legal power, politics, and sites for particular kinds of struggle. As legal theorist Costas Douzinas[13] summarizes, human rights denote a diverse group of constitutional, legal, judicial, academic, and popular texts and commentaries; legal, political, and cultural institutions; governmental and nongovernmental agencies, and personnel and the campaigns in which they are waged. Rights, a relational legal category, are linked to the human as a moral one that gives these a special, if not transcendent, value in liberal ideology. As a topic of jurisprudence, they constitute a morally-inflected ideal that serves as a "trump card" in political argument. Thus they can and often are deployed cynically for political purposes. Human rights have become a major strategy for resisting public and private domination and exploitation; they are central to a long history of rebellion, resistance, new articulations of injustice, and new understandings of freedom. At once vehicles of law, they are also the primary source of its limit, restricting its force and its positivity.

Douzinas provides a passionate and ambiguous account of the place of human rights in the constitution of a new world order in the first decade of the new millennium, asking: "[A]re human rights an effective defensive tool against domination and oppression or are they the ideological gloss of an emerging empire?"[14] He clearly believes that human rights are inherently contradictory and thus, paradoxically, both, but he devotes more energy to illustrating the latter than exploring the former. Deploying semiotic, deconstructionist, psychoanalytic, and poststructuralist theory he explains the pursuit of human rights by reference to the endless pursuit of a human desire for recognition, respect, and self-realization in negotiations of identity that continuously fall short of fully embracing (most of) us while providing compensation for ever greater socio-legal subjection.

Indian legal philosopher Upendra Baxi[15] articulates two current concepts of human rights: a "modern" paradigm based on classic Enlightenment ideas of human essentialism and reason, and a "contemporary" variant marked by its diversity, pluralism, and multiculturalism. The dominant ideological narrative maintains that human rights are the fruits of a peculiarly Western tradition of philosophy. Baxi finds this genealogy limited and self-serving, but convincing to the extent that the evil occasioned by the "modern" paradigm of human rights may be attributed to Enlightenment liberalism as an ideology of exclusion that provided the imperialist West with a rationale for both declassifying huge groups of disadvantaged others from the category of those who possessed rights and a moral legitimation for racism and colonialism. Moreover, it enabled the perpetuation of an imperialist ideology in which human rights are a continuing "gift from the West to the rest" in which others must continually show themselves to be worthy of "our" largesse. Instead, Baxi insists that we recognize people in struggle as the originary authors of human rights considered as an open and morally imaginative practice.

Postcolonial legal theorist, Balakrishnan Rajagopal,[16] for example, explores how international legal institutions of human rights have been shaped historically by social contexts of colonialism, as well as by anti-colonial nationalist movements. He advocates closer attention to new social movements as alternative sites of resistance that provide new models of social justice outside of modern human rights frameworks. Protesting international law's promotion of human rights as the only appropriate route to emancipation and social justice, he shows how international human rights law has repeatedly developed so as to contain resistance movements and challenges to Western hegemony while enabling and extending new forms of governance over Third World masses envisioned through colonial tropes of fear and loathing.

Nonetheless, Rajagopal shows that some of these new anti-globalization movements have had some influence even within UN rights-based institutions.[17] His critique could be developed as a critical cultural study of rights if it were to explore the ways in which these "other" movements have translated rights concepts for new ends, pluralizing the rights field, particularly via the "turn to culture" which, he acknowledges, has put new emphasis on identity, territory, autonomy, and alternative understandings of development.[18] His position is also challenged by the near global ratification of the Declaration of the Rights of Indigenous Peoples in 2007, which has put those "place-based, concrete strategies for survival of individuals and communities in the Third World ... aimed at building radical alternatives to the received models of markets and democracy"[19] he champions squarely into the global human rights arena, along with regional rights charters and many national constitutions, particularly in Latin America, which have enabled cultural difference to assume a new role in a transnational subaltern politics.

Clearly human rights laws are the fulcrum of a pervasive, powerful, and authoritative normative discourse that requires the same powerful instruments of analysis that a critical cultural studies brings to bear on other discourses. Critical theories of law have long recognized law's legitimation functions, its cultural role in constituting the social realities we recognize. Human rights, as expressed in canonical texts, as talk, as a way of thinking, and as a form of practice, might be approached *as* culture to the extent that this discourse entails certain dominant constructions of self and sociality, and specific modes of agency. As a field of law, human rights constitute a worldview and structuring discourse that shapes the way we apprehend the world. Legal discourse provides a powerful imaginary, and the human rights imaginary appears to have increasing influence at multiple scales of jurisdiction and influence, shaping the practices of an ever greater range of actors, institutions, and agencies.

Historically structured and locally interpreted, human rights law provides means and fora for legitimating and contesting privileged narratives and the social hierarchies they support in practices of articulation in which hegemonic and oppositional strategies both constitute and reconfigure each other. Social worlds need to be represented, performatively expressed, and institutionally inscribed; human rights provide authoritative rhetorical means, media, and arenas for articulating improved human worlds and incorporating new visions of society, but they can also be deployed to ratify new forms of oppressive power. There is now a large body of law and society literature that considers the prospects and limits of legal rights as the basis for political struggle, much of this coming from critical reflection upon the civil rights struggle in the United States.[20] Liberal rights politics that interpret Enlightenment equality principles have engaged issues of sameness and difference as they challenge invisible norms that operate as formidable forms of privilege. Civil and political rights, however, are only one area of human rights, and movements to achieve economic, social, and cultural rights must also concern us. These latter are less likely to privilege litigation strategies, and are more likely to involve civil society or nongovernmental organizations (NGOs) who engage mass and digital media to shape public opinion, shame corporations, and sway legislatures.

Critical scholarship on international human rights is far more eclectic, far less sanguine, and less focused upon their efficacy in achieving progressive social change. Baxi,[21] for instance, is at pains to illustrate the different ways in which human rights are used and understood, insisting on the *radical contingency* of "human rights futures" that share no definite *telos* or principle of gradual realization. Indeed, he feels that the future of human rights lies in such diverse phenomena as the overproduction of human rights norms, the repressive as well as emancipatory potential of these norms, and the effects of the globalized market. Cultural diversity will and should play a guiding role in shaping human rights futures, which must expand well beyond the guarantee of bourgeois rights.

Although human rights law provides vehicles to constrain state power, human rights discourse is also frequently politicized and deployed for state ends. Not surprisingly, the historical development of human rights reflects Cold War priorities and animosities; its contemporary deployment advances neoliberal governmental agendas according to Douzinas.

> Governmental actions in the international arenas are dictated by national interest and political considerations, and morality enters the stage always late, when the principle invoked happens to condemn the actions of a political adversary. When human rights and national interest coincide, governments become their greatest champions. But this is the exception ... A state that adopts the international treaties can claim to be a human rights state, turning human rights into a ploy for state legitimacy. Natural and human rights were conceived as a tool against the despotism of power and the arrogance of wealth. Their co-optation by governments means that they have lost much of their critical force and their initial aim and role has been reversed.[22]

In the United States, government officials, legislators, NGO leaders, and media celebrities have adopted human rights as the ideological banner under which both culture wars and international political battles have been fought.[23] Douzinas sees human rights as an invaluable American ideological weapon that has enabled the US to assume the moral high ground in international affairs, especially since 1989 when these became "the only ideology in town."[24] Highjacked by governments to form the basis for new forms of colonialism in which an ideology of the rich is imposed on the poor, he still believes that a residue of transcendence remains in human rights discourse for the protests, resistances, and struggles of others.

Far less optimistically, Baxi traces the emergence of what he deems "human rights markets", entailed by the need for activists and NGOs to compete for scarce resources in arenas in which human rights investors, producers, and consumers must be identified and targeted, given widespread media desensitization and scarcities of funding. Moreover, he postulates the emergence of "an alternative paradigm of human rights" in which institutions of global capital—from the World Trade Organization (WTO) and International Monetry Fund (IMF) to multinational corporations—use human rights vocabularies to justify corporate well-being and dignity even when these entail "gross and flagrant violation of human rights of actually existing human beings and communities".[25] Such trade-related, market-friendly neoliberal human rights threaten to foreclose "human-rights oriented, redistributionist governance practices" and the progressive realization of economic, social and cultural rights.[26]

In a cogent argument for the relevance of humanities scholarship and deconstructionist theory to the study of human rights as a global discourse and movement,

Pheng Cheah argues that contemporary celebrations of cosmopolitanism radically discount the degree to which the discourses of human rights have become contaminated by the inequities of global capitalism and the capture of state agencies by neoliberal economic policies.[27] The World Bank, transnational advocacy networks, and the elite civil society of NGOs are all similarly indicted as undermining the state as the proper guardian of social justice by Cheah, for whom globalization appears to be a singular and totalizing force. Despite his emphasis on the humanities, his case studies of economic elites, women's rights, and migrant workers' treatment in China and Southeast Asia use sociological and anthropological theory when considering the interlinked concepts of humanity and inhumanity at work in legal practice. While critical of the concepts of universalist transcendence central to liberal rights ideologies, Cheah expresses desire for a human rights that transcends the capitalist world system; he privileges the modern state as its only possible progenitor.

Although state activity continues to be subject to global scrutiny by international actors, and states are clearly primary actors in international governance, human rights activity and monitoring increasingly encompasses a wider field of agency. A transnationally networked field of institutionalized advocacy involving NGOs, development banks, aid organizations, and indigenous peoples has emerged in the last two decades in which the discourse of human rights is deployed at multiple scales to design, influence, shape, and resist projects and programmes implemented by many different kinds of private and public actors. Human rights practitioners are increasingly professionals who operate within a political economy that has its own forms of expertise, values particular forms of social capital, engages in particular forms of subject formation, and creates its own fields of knowledge and power. As such, it is a field that lends itself to the Foucauldian analytic lens of governmentality studies that has been so fruitfully taken up in cultural studies.[28]

In *Transnational America* for example, Inderpal Grewal explores how circulations of goods, social movements, and discourse in the 1990s created new transnational subjects.[29] Neoliberalism, she argues, was constituted through assemblages of disciplinary power and governmental technologies legitimated through a nationalist discourse that produced subjects and agencies far outside US borders. "America" has long been a symbol of freedom and democratic rights as well as imperial power, but only recently, it seems, have rights discourses been conjoined with consumer culture to convince others that they are disenfranchised so as to recruit them as subject to new forms of asymmetrical internationalism, corporate power, and white nationalism.[30] Grewal's ambitious (and often unwieldy) analysis traces the increasing use of human rights as a pedagogic discourse of transnational tutelage, in which the capacity to exercise "choice" held by those in market-oriented societies is continuously distinguished from the oppressions of others who lack human rights and need to be actively reconstructed as appropriate rights holders through technologies of knowledge production.

In this work of "managing the crisis of continuing inequalities,"[31] NGOs became transnational instruments of governmentality, using the discourse of human rights to instrumentalize new regimes of good governance, construct new apparatuses as indices of population welfare, and produce new subjects in need of rescue, charity, and care so they might see themselves as autonomous individuals. In the process, "America" was positioned as the site for authoritative condemnation of rights "abuses," and constructed as the centre of utmost freedom and rights, and preeminently privileged in adjudicating their lack elsewhere.[32] Human rights thus became governmental tools for managing populations—used, for example, to decide which persons were appropriate to be granted refugee asylum. Human rights legitimated the generation of new knowledges by transnational NGOs while an ethic of humanitarian concern animated new technologies for combining geopolitics and biopolitics.

The World Bank also deploys human rights for biopolitical intervention in former socialist and less developed countries, Anne Orford[33] shows, through pedagogical packages designed to teach values of market capitalism, efficiency, and approved modes of compliance. Nutrition, youth development, reproductive health, disease management, and sanitation are all issue areas that bring multilateral institutions, NGOs, and activists into huge enterprises for the control, normalization, and policing of the poor to effectively transform them into appropriate forms of human capital for new markets. Law professor David Kennedy also asserts that contemporary humanitarianism has become a new form of industry in which governments, armies, NGOs, and erstwhile activists forge new combat alliances using the vehicles of neoliberal governmentality to further "ruleship" and military policy-making under contemporary conditions of empire.[34] As Douzinas concurs:

> ... it looks like an imperial officer corps and bureaucracy is emerging ... a new professional class, the "humanitarians" or "internationals." ... The group includes the usual suspects: human rights activists, lawyers, international civil servants, NGO operators and assorted do-gooders and all those whose task is to spread the principles of the new world order, if necessary, by force ... the task is now to consolidate and generalize this project of osmosis between humanitarians, the military and politicians and turn it into a world ideology.[35]

Sharply diverging from Kennedy's complacent pragmatism, however, Douzinas believes that human rights continue to "work in the gap between ideal nature and law, or between real people and universal abstractions."[36] The so-called "universal ethics" of professional humanitarians who have turned the priorities of American elites into global principles that generate governmental legitimacy represents a peculiar new form of hegemonic enterprise. Nonetheless, like Baxi, he would:

> ... insist against realists, pragmatists and the ideologues of power that the energy necessary for protection, horizontal proliferation, and vertical expansion of human rights comes from below, from those whose lives have been blighted by oppression ... Human rights professionals, whether radical or pragmatic, are at best ancillary to this task, which cannot be delegated.[37]

Anthropological Studies of Human Rights: Practice and Identity

Exploring human rights' structurations and governmentalities is significant work for cultural studies scholars who must, also, however, recognize that such configurations of power face challenges and limits from alternative histories, imaginaries, and moral economies of value and solidarity as these figure in local struggles. From a cultural studies perspective, human rights can never be approached exclusively as ideology, but only through the social life of rights' textuality in fields of political practice. To paraphrase Toby Miller, while marrying approaches from the humanities and social sciences, we can afford neither abstracted empiricism nor grand moralism in the service of critique; a critical cultural study of human rights must marry the interpretive strengths of textual analysis with the distributional concerns of political or cultural economy, the scepticism of critical theory, and the anti-foundationalism of poststructural philosophies while considering networks, technologies, and traditions.[38] Moreover, we need to link characteristic forms of interpretive practice and agency with specific modes of interpellation and subject formation.

Towards this end, sociologist Fuyuki Kurasawa provides an "action-based" approach that reconfigures human rights as the products of particular human practices rather than the application of a universal normative system. He argues that we must move beyond philosophical normativities, cosmopolitan ethics, the endless work of justifying human rights frameworks, an emphasis on institutions, and empiricist preoccupations with civil society networks.[39] Proposing "critical substantivism" as an approach that "mak[es] sense of the realities of participants involved in the social labor of global justice and the meaning they give to this labor,"[40] he suggests a critical cultural sociology of human rights that focuses on practice.[41] Practice is understood as both structured and structuring, shaping larger institutional fields through interpretive practices that critically rework historical, social, and cultural systems of thought and action.[42]

Five activities enact global justice and thereby produce human rights in his study: bearing witness, forgiveness, foresight, aid, and solidarity. Each of these projects of social labor constitutes a form of struggle that inevitably encounters obstacles that lead to the repetitive enactment of a "repertoire of social tasks" that thereby forms a "mode of practice."[43] In the labour of "bearing witness," for example, actors find means of overcoming silence, incomprehension, indifference, and forgetting, and thereby *produce* human rights as social capacity. Although he intends to provide an "interpretively thick" explanation of what actors are doing when they advance human rights, it is doubtful that human rights practices are as unified, intentional, and seamlessly productive as the rather tidy social processes that Kurasawa outlines. Unfortunately, the practices he explores are sociologically quite "thin" because they are presented as if they are engaged in by socially undifferentiated actors. We get little understanding of the historical contexts that shape their agency or the self-understandings they bring to human rights activities. Despite an early acknowledgment that "relations of power structure the fields of action in which modes of practice operate,"[44] the volume largely ignores such structurations. How, we might wonder, do such practices shape, influence, or transform the social identities of actors in the world thereafter?

Legal anthropologists have long seen law as a site for cultural construction and social struggle in the constitution of both individual and group identities.[45] Even as local identities and concerns are translated and transformed in legal language, people put the law's idioms, categories, limits, and opportunity structures to work in their own struggles; rights function ambivalently in fostering and constraining the development of community and individual identities. As anthropologist Mark Goodale suggests, as "one of the most consequential of transnational regimes," human rights have both instrumental and ideological aspects:

> A political economy of human rights discourse is one that studies the ways in which human rights ideas and practices—which are rendered discursively inseparable in specific social contexts—have become preeminently constitutive, so that collective identity, social meanings, and personhood cannot be understood in other terms even when—perhaps *especially* when—moves are made to suggest alternatives ... [it is] to recognize that "the work of [human rights] is necessarily grammatical: naming, constructing and positioning the [normative] and doing so in a way which builds social relations of power and knowledge" ... rather than as international human rights doctrine presupposes, *discovers* them within the natural order of things.[46]

Douzinas shares this view of human rights practices as socially generative, suggesting that every exercise of rights potentially rearranges social hierarchy, opening new vistas, that "if petrified, becomes itself an external limitation that must be again overcome ..."[47] Legally produced boundaries are always contested and, "in this sense, freedom can be enhanced by the potential of rights to extend the limits of the social and to expand and redefine self and group identities."[48]

The last decades of the twentieth century witnessed a dramatic increase in negotiations between social groups phrased in the language of rights, leading anthropologists especially to suggest that philosophical and theoretical studies of rights needed to be augmented with contextual studies of rights processes and the power relations at work in legal constructions of culture, tradition, and community.[49] Anthropologists consider the role of rights discourse in essentializing social categories and fixing identities for legal purposes, a point which is still underappreciated by those for whom locating imagined communities and allegations of the invention of tradition constitute self-sufficient critiques.[50] Popular terms such as "strategic essentialism," for instance, may denote an instrumentality that fails to do justice to the constitutive social work of human rights discourse and practice. Some of the "cultures" caught up in rights processes may indeed come to exist after rights claims are made on their behalf: "[T]o the extent that claimants are compelled to use a language of rights in pursuit of what they need or want, and to portray themselves as certain kinds of persons, when these may be alien to their self-understandings, it is evident that rights discourses are not ethically unambiguous or neutral."[51] We should explore the possibility that self-understandings and community identities may become constitutively transformed by rights projects, yielding new and different kinds of persons and sociality, particularly under neoliberal pressures.

Just as promising for a cultural studies of rights is the anthropological call to move beyond Western philosophical discourse and critical theory to consider human rights as a more dialectical and intercultural process of *articulation*—exploring how local concerns, worldviews, categories, and understandings shape the way putatively universal categories of rights are implemented, resisted, and transformed.[52] In these processes, claimants become involved in transnational political connectivities even and especially as they struggle to assert the significance of local specificities. Refusing to posit the relationship between rights and culture oppositionally, Jane Cowan et al. suggest, anthropologists now see the dominant discourse of human rights as one that incorporates:

> ... both universal rights premised on sameness and an awareness—increasingly even a celebration—of cultural differences, making exhaustive debates forcing the "choice" between universalism and relativism seem both dog-eared and dogmatic ... Just as there are no singular social cultures with fixed values and meanings, there is no unitary field of human rights with absolute certainties ... Both are fields of creative interchange and contestation ... There are no societies without access to human rights, and it is precisely those whom are most marginalized and stigmatized because of their differences whom are most likely to need the political tools that human rights provide. States have, through forced assimilation policies, long made sameness the price for granting rights and when they do, rights based on difference may be emancipatory. On the other hand, when states insist upon particular forms of difference being calcified and performed according to rigid scripts, they may also violate rights ... Both innate cultural differences and abstract universal principles are fictions that can be rhetorically deployed opportunistically in political tactics and to obscure other interests and further other agendas.[53]

Conceiving of rights as authoritative texts and key symbols inevitably interpreted and deployed in particular contexts, many ethnographers now recognize legal processes as practices of critical hermeneutics in which law (despite its positivist tendencies) must continually readjust to local realities, social change, and new demands.[54] They have chosen to explore the proliferation of mutually transformative conversations between local worlds of meaning and global ones that constitute a new transnational *culture* of human rights practice.

Anthropologists engaged in fieldwork in the 1990s increasingly found human rights to be a transnational discursive framework deeply imbricated in local political and moral practice; advancing human rights regimes were interacting with indigenous cultural forms and local interpretations to produce dialectically reciprocal transformations. New conceptions of rights are inevitably interpreted through locally relevant and sometimes traditional senses of obligation, just as they are tied up with philosophies, histories, and utopian constructs usually honed in the histories of former colonizing powers. Novel justice imaginaries are forged when Europe is provincialized and Enlightenment conceptual vocabularies encounter, challenge, and accommodate other regimes of meaning and value. Thus they suggest that we need to understand human rights "in the vernacular"[55] recognizing that "human rights must be both theorized and legitimated *in terms of* the groundedness of social practices, those mundane (yet often transformative) occurrences of ... the 'practice of everyday life'."[56] Moreover, we might argue that any consideration of the "vernacularization" of human rights must also attend to the multiplicity of other normative and ideological frameworks (environmental sustainability, human capabilities, neoliberalism, indigeneity) with which these are increasingly enmeshed. We cannot lose sight of the global political economic contexts in which human rights practices emerge and take shape; neither, however, should we assume that hegemonies are fixed or always already in place.

Some Cultural Studies' Human Rights' Futures

I have suggested that the cultural studies of human rights might develop more profitably through greater attention to and in dialogue with a range of interdisciplinary work on human rights that adopts similar methods, and shares theoretical orientations with work in cultural studies more generally, particularly scholarship that attempts to develop analyses of emerging cultures of rights in transnational fields of politics and in the global cultural economy. One area of potential departure was signaled by George Yudice in *The Expediency of Culture*,[57] when he suggested that communications and cultural studies scholars need to understand the growing significance of "culture as a resource," a paradigm shift which posed fundamental challenges to scholarly understandings of culture. To paraphrase his thesis, in contemporary political economies and expressive political practice, culture has become an object of new economic attention and policy insight, as well as the rhetorical basis for new forms of social struggle. This prescient insight still needs to be theoretically elaborated, institutionally grounded, situated in a larger field of international cultural policy, and positioned in the emerging field of transnational cultural studies. Moreover, we need to more fully understand the legal conditions of culture's emergence as a resource, and the political agencies through which new fields of cultural rights have assumed prominence so as to consider the conditions under which new political economies of culture might do justice to new forms of social struggle as well as new forms of capital accumulation.

Emerging social justice struggles increasingly make assertions on cultural grounds, possessive claims to culture are proliferating,[58] and cultural traditions provide the basis for new forms of political and social initiative, industry, and investment around the world.[59] Cultural rights claims are unquestionably tied to changing patterns of global capital accumulation.[60] Culture has acquired a new value in rural, sustainable, and rights-based development projects and consumption practices. New forms of ethno-development, including cultural tourism and the cultivation of culturally distinctive export goods, for example, are understood by diverse actors to have the capacity to foster rural economic revitalization and secure sustainable livelihoods.[61]

Neoliberal governmentality profoundly "shapes cultural realms in the production and affirmation of diversity through the commodification of difference"[62] as well as in its investments in creative classes, creative industries, and its newest subjects, "the creatives." Its mandates are interpreted—worked by the subjects it enables[63] through and with locally relevant systems of meaning. As an analytic category, neoliberalism may be approached "as an assemblage of technologies, techniques, and practices that are appropriated selectively"[64] in contexts in which people may also become more conscious of their rights and more reflective about what makes them uniquely human.

A critical cultural studies of human rights attentive to culture as a resource might address both the local needs and desires of actors engaged in transnationally linked social movements that inspire claims to cultural "goods" as well as the neoliberal interpellation of market-based subjectivities that seek to naturalize possessive relationships to culture as a development asset, while interrogating their relationship. To pose just a few questions likely to emerge on this terrain: Under what circumstances do neoliberal desires to locate social capital and invest in its (market-based) futures fit within, come up against, or become transformed by rights-based struggles? When do new forms of property introduced into cultural spheres simply extend the logic of the commodity, and when do these further new forms of political citizenship or autonomy? Are self-governing market-oriented subjects of neoliberalism eclipsing modern individual human rights holders, or are new hybrid subjects emerging? How does the recognition of collective proprietary cultural rights enable new forms of subjectivity to be expressed? Culture is doing distinctive and different kinds of work in global markets, neoliberal governmentalities, indigenist movements, and environmentalist regimes to name only a few contemporary fields of transnational power and knowledge. Exploring the "friction"[65] produced when attachments to cultural expression, cultural work, cultural industries, and cultural traditions encounter, transform or are transformed by human rights practices suggests new opportunities for critical cultural studies scholarship.

Notes

[1] Thomas Hylland Eriksen, "Between Universalism and Relativism: A Critique of the UNESCO Concept of Culture," in *Culture and Rights: Anthropological Perspectives*, ed. Jane Cowan, Marie-Benedicte Dembour, and Richard Wilson (Cambridge: Cambridge University Press, 2001), 127–48.
[2] Bruce Robbins and Elsa Stamatopolou, "Reflections on Culture and Cultural Rights," *South Atlantic Quarterly* 103 (2004): 419–34.
[3] Jane Cowan, Marie-Benedicte Dembour and Richard Wilson, "Introduction," in *Culture and Rights: Anthropological Perspectives*, eds. Jane Cowan, Marie-Benedicte Dembour and Richard Wilson (Cambridge: Cambridge University Press, 2001), 1–26.
[4] Stuart Cunningham, "Cultural Studies from the Viewpoint of Cultural Policy," in *Critical Cultural Policy Studies: A Reader*, ed. Justin Lewis and Toby Miller (Malden, MA: Blackwell Publishing, 2003), 13–22; Stuart Cunningham, "The Creative Industries after Cultural Policy: A Genealogy and Some Possible Preferred Futures," *International Journal of Cultural Studies* 7 (2004): 105–15; John McMurria, "Moby Dick, Cultural Policy and the Geographies and Geopolitics of Cultural Labor," *International Journal of Cultural Studies* 12 (2009): 237–56.
[5] Justin Lewis and Toby Miller, ed., *Critical Cultural Policy Studies* (Malden, MA: Blackwell Publishing, 2003); Toby Miller and George Yudice, *Cultural Policy* (Thousand Oaks, CA: Sage Publications, 2002).
[6] Tony Bennett and Colin Mercer, "Improving Research and International Cooperation for Cultural Policy," in *Commentaries: Recasting Cultural Policies, Our Creative Diversity* (UNESCO World Commission for Culture and Development, 1998).
[7] Kevin Robins, "Transnational Cultural Policy and European Cosmpolitanism," *Cultural Politics* 3 (2008): 147–74.
[8] Richard Johnson, "What is Cultural Studies Anyway?," *Social Text* 16 (1987): 38–80.

[9] Arjun Appadurai, "Global Ethnoscapes: Notes and Queries for a Transnational Anthropology," in *Recapturing Anthropology*, ed. Richard J. Fox (Santa Fe, NM: School of American Research, 1991), 191–210.
[10] Mark Goodale, "Introduction: Human Rights and Anthropology," in *Human Rights: An Anthropological Reader*, ed. Mark Goodale (Chichester: Wiley-Blackwell, 2009), 1–20.
[11] George Yudice, *The Expediency of Culture* (Durham, NC: Duke University Press, 2003).
[12] Vijayendra Rao and Michael Walton, ed., *Culture and Public Action* (Stanford, CA: Stanford University Press, 2004).
[13] Costas Douzinas, *Human Rights and Empire: The Political Philosophy of Cosmopolitanism* (Abingdon: Routledge-Cavendish, 2007).
[14] Douzinas, 7.
[15] Upendra Baxi, *The Future of Human Rights* (New Delhi: Oxford University Press, 2002).
[16] Balakrishnan Rajagopal, *International Law From Below* (Cambridge: Cambridge University Press, 2003).
[17] Ibid., 158–9.
[18] Ibid., 165–6.
[19] Ibid., 170.
[20] See, for example, Gerard Rosenburg, *The Hollow Hope: Can Courts Bring about Social Change?* (Chicago, IL: University of Chicago Press, 1991) and Stuart Scheingold, *The Politics of Rights* (New Haven, CT: Yale University Press, 1974).
[21] Baxi.
[22] Douzinas, 24.
[23] Ibid., 27.
[24] Ibid., 33.
[25] Baxi, 132; also see John Erni, "Human Rights in the Neoliberal Imagination: Mapping the New Sovereignties," *Cultural Studies* 23 (2009): 417–36.
[26] Baxi, 139.
[27] Pheng Cheah, *Inhuman Conditions: On Cosmopolitanism and Human Rights* (Cambridge, MA: Harvard University Press, 2006).
[28] See, for example, Clive Barnett, "Culture, Government and Spatiality: Reassessing the 'Foucault Effect' in Cultural Policy," *International Journal of Cultural Studies* 2 (1999): 369–97; Clive Barnett et al., "The Elusive Subjects of Neo-Liberalism: Beyond the Analytics of Governmentality," *Cultural Studies* 22 (2008): 624–53; Tony Bennett, "Culture and Governmentality," in *Foucault, Cultural Studies and Governmentality*, ed. Jack Bratich, Jeremy Packer and Cameron McCarthy (Albany, NY: SUNY Press, 2003), 47–62.
[29] Inderpal Grewal, *Transnational America: Feminisms, Diasporas, Neoliberalisms* (Durham, NH: Duke University Press, 2005).
[30] Ibid., 9.
[31] Ibid., 11.
[32] Ibid., 157.
[33] Anne Orford, "Beyond Harmonisation: Trade, Human Rights and the Economy of Sacrifice," in *International Law and its Others*, ed. Anne Orford (Cambridge: Cambridge University Press, 2006), 156–96.
[34] David Kennedy, *The Dark Side of Virtue* (Princeton, NJ: Princeton University Press, 2004).
[35] Douzinas, 64–5.
[36] Ibid., 65.
[37] Ibid., 66.
[38] Toby Miller, "Introducing Screening Cultural Studies," *Continuum* 7 (1994): 11–44.
[39] Fuyuki Kurasawa, *Global Justice: Human Rights as Practices* (Cambridge: Cambridge University Press, 2007).
[40] Ibid., 8.
[41] Ibid., 11.

[42] Ibid., 12.
[43] Ibid., 12.
[44] Ibid., 15.
[45] Elizabeth Mertz, "Legal Loci and Places in the Heart: Community and Identity in Sociolegal Studies," *Law and Society Review* 28 (1994): 971–92; Rosemary J. Coombe, "Intellectual Property in Neoliberal Regimes of Governmentality: Community Subjects and their Rights," in *The Making and Unmaking of Intellectual Property*, ed. Mario Biagioli, Martha Woodmansee and Peter Jaszi (Chicago, IL: University of Chicago Press, 2010), in press.
[46] Mark Goodale, "Toward a Critical Anthropology of Human Rights," *Current Anthropology* 47 (2006): 485–511, internal citations omitted.
[47] Douzinas, 13.
[48] Ibid., 13.
[49] Cowan, Dembour and Wilson, 21. While most anthropologists have moved away from the relativist, functionalist and holistic accounts of culture that dominated the discipline's early colonial period as well as its mid-century rejection of human rights universalism, legal anthropologists have been particularly aware of the origins of the culture concept in comparative law and attuned to law and legal discourse as a socially and politically constitutive force; the anthropology of human rights is a relatively recent subfield that often seeks to "site" culture as it is deployed in diverse struggles.
[50] Rosemary J. Coombe, "Owning Culture: Political Economies of Community Subjects and their Properties," in *Ownership and Appropriation*, ed. Mark Busse and Veronica Strang (Oxford: Berg Publishers, 2010), 105–27.
[51] Cowan, Dembour and Wilson, 11.
[52] Mark Goodale, "Locating Rights, Envisioning Law Between the Global and the Local," in *The Practice of Human Rights: Tracking Law between the Global and the Local*, ed. Sally Engle Merry and Mark Goodale (Cambridge: Cambridge University Press, 2007), 1–38; Sally Engle Merry, "Changing Rights, Changing Culture," in *Culture and Rights: Anthropological Perspectives*, ed. Jane Cowan, Marie-Benedicte Dembour and Richard Wilson (Cambridge: Cambridge University Press, 2001), 31–55; Sally Engle Merry, "Transnational Human Rights and Local Activism: Mapping the Middle," *American Anthropologist* 108 (2006): 38–51; Shannon Speed, *Rights in Rebellion: Indigenous Struggle and Human Rights in Chiapas* (Stanford, CA: Stanford University Press, 2008).
[53] Cowan, Dembour and Wilson, 5–6.
[54] Ibid., 6.
[55] Goodale, 2009, 13.
[56] Ibid., 14.
[57] Yudice.
[58] Michael Brown, "Heritage Trouble: Recent Work on the Protection of Intangible Cultural Property," *International Journal of Cultural Property* 12 (2005): 40–61; Rosemary J. Coombe, "The Changing Purview of Cultural Property and its Politics," *Annual Review of Law and Social Science* 5 (2009): 393–412.
[59] John Comaroff and Jean Comaroff, *Ethnicity Inc.* (Chicago, IL: University of Chicago Press, 2009).
[60] Rosemary J. Coombe, Steven Schnoor and Mohsen al Attar Ahmed, "Bearing Cultural Distinction: Informational Capital and New Expectations for Intellectual Property," *University of California Davis Law Review* 40 (2007): 891–917; Katherine Verdery and Caroline Humphrey, ed., *Property in Question: Value Transformations in the Global Economy* (Oxford: Berg Publishers, 2004).
[61] Arjun Appadurai, "The Capacity to Aspire: Culture and the Terms of Recognition," in Rao and Walton: 59–85; Rosemary J. Coombe and Nicole Aylwin, "Bordering Diversity and Desire: Using Intellectual Property to Mark Place-based Products," *Environment and Planning A* (forthcoming); Jonathan Ensor, "Linking Rights and Culture," in *Reinventing*

Development: Translating Rights-Based Approaches from Theory into Practice, ed. Paul Gready and Jonathan Ensor (London: Zed Books, 2005), 254–77; Sarah A. Radcliffe, ed., *Culture and Development in a Globalizing World: Geographies, Actors, and Paradigms* (London and New York: Routledge, 2006); Jan Rath, *Tourism, Ethnic Diversity and the City* (London: Routledge, 2007).

[62] Thomas Perreault and Patricia Martin, "Geographies of Neoliberalism in Latin America," *Environment and Planning A* 37(2) (2005): 191–201.

[63] Liz Bondi and Nina Laurie, "Introduction," in *Working the Spaces of Neoliberalism*, ed. Nina Laurie and Liz Bondi (Malden, MA: Blackwell Publishing, 2005), 1–8.

[64] John Clarke, "Living With/in and Without Neoliberalism," *Focaal–European Journal of Anthropology* 51 (2008): 135–47.

[65] Anna Tsing, *Friction: An Ethnography of Global Connection* (Princeton, NJ: Princeton University Press, 2005).

Immanent Law and the Juridical: Toward a Liberative Ontology of Human Rights

Hans Skott-Myhre & Donato Tarulli

This article elaborates an ontology of human rights as immanent potential produced outside of modernist frameworks. We begin with a consideration of the political and juridical subject of human rights, the subjectus, whose relation to sovereign law is one of submission and supplication. We then examine three registers of "the law" that bear on the question of the subject, with a view to highlighting the distinction between law as a meditative, autopoietically sustained sovereign force, and as immanent production. Building on this conception of law as pure productivity, we propose an ontology of the subjectum for whom human rights are idiosyncratically produced acts of becoming or, in Spinozist terms, expressions of creative life force. While state and juridical forms may, through codification and re-presentation, attempt to contain and turn such open-ended possibility to their own ends, the material force of the subjectum, through its immanent expression of rights, carries the liberative potential to collapse sovereign force into its own expressive capacities. It is proposed, accordingly, that rights neither require nor depend on the ability to petition the state for legal status, but rather are produced within the forms of daily life of the multitude, that internally diversified social subject whose constitution and political action is premised neither on identity nor on appeals to sovereign power, but rather on what its singularities have in common.

> When I was back there in seminary school
> There was a person there
> Who put forth the proposition
> That you can petition the Lord with prayer
> Petition the lord with prayer?
> You cannot petition the lord with prayer!
>   Jim Morrison[1]

We began this writing as a constituted set of dualities, the two of us as certain kinds of subjects. In the moment of writing we are posited as an epistemological contestation between that which we are proposed to be and that which we are precisely propositionally not. In this, we found ourselves produced and producing ourselves as male, adult, academic, Canadian and American, rural and urban—among other oppositional categories. Such a manner of writing delineates a certain positionality of the subject that we found ourselves subjected to as well as constituted within. The coordinates of such a location concomitantly produce a set of relations to the subject that we wish to engage—that is, the subject posited in relation to the discourse of rights.

It would be our contention that rights begin with the production of the subject. Indeed, it is only with the eruption of the subject that rights and the concomitant contestation for the distribution of productive power inherent within the assertions of force epistemologically constructed as democracy take flight. Such a subject as explosive force was from its inception inherently corrosive to regimes of sovereignty produced through discipline, control, and appropriation. As Hardt and Negri have pointed out, this characteristic of the force of production, manifested through the earliest forms of the humanist self, constituted a radically new and accelerated mode of creativity that had infinite liberative capacity.[2] It is precisely this capacity that systems of sovereignty have sought to both appropriate and discipline to the ends of modern economic formations. This contestation between liberative creative capacity and disciplinary modes of capture and appropriation, we would argue, has produced two forms of the subject that we are interested in here: the modernist subject produced through disciplinary forms of sovereignty, and the radically idiosyncratic subject of infinite creative autopoiesis, referred to as the *multitude*.[3]

Subject as *Subjectus*

To unpack the distinction between these two subjects and their relation to the question of rights, it is necessary to investigate briefly the constitutive relations of sovereignty, freedom, and power held as both transcendental and latent capacities in the production of the entity 'subject.' In his essay, "Citizen Subject," Balibar asks:

> "Who is the subject?" The question is not about the *subjectum* but about the *subjectus*, he who is subjected ... the subject as an individual or a person submitted to the exercise of a power, whose model is, first of all, political, and whose concept is juridical. Not the subject inasmuch as it is opposed to the predicate or to the object but the one referred to by Bossuet's thesis: "*All men are born subjects and the paternal authority that accustoms them to obeying accustoms them at the same time to having only one chief.*"[4]

Following Balibar, then, the *subjectus* is a particular sort of political and juridical subject produced and refined over seventeen centuries, from Rome to the development of monarchical Europe. *Subjectus* is a term that:

refers to *subjection* or *submission*, i.e. the fact that a (generally) human person (man, woman or child) is *subjected to* the more or less absolute, more or less legitimate authority of a superior power, e.g., a "sovereign." This sovereign being may be another human or supra-human, or an 'inner' sovereign or master, or even simply a transcendent (impersonal) *law*.[5]

Like the characters in monologic literary genres, whose truths are always subordinated to the author's "ultimate semantic authority," the subject as *subjectus* is defined in terms of its submission to an overarching authorial vision, its autonomy, creativity, and freedom (that is, its status as *subjectum*) essentially closed off by the unitary, monologic voice of an omniscient other/self.[6] This subject is a finalized subject, a subject who fully coincides with the heteronomous outside—a subject with no remainder, who enjoys no existential surplus or "breathing space" from which to undermine, challenge, or simply surprise the author-sovereign.[7] As Hardt and Negri have pointed out, this subject is positioned in such a way as to mediate the flows and contestations of force between the absolute productivity of what Spinoza refers to as *conatus*, or the immanent striving of each body to persevere through the capacity to act, and the transcendent systems that would contain and direct such action.[8]

Such a subject sits outside the law and, as in Kafka's parable, petitions for entry. Of course, entry into the law is impossible for the *subjectus*, because, as Luhmann has argued, the law operates on an autopoietic logic—a logic fully contained by the law—and as such radically excludes the *subjectus*.[9] In other words, the law produces the functions of the law and produces itself through the perturbations of the petitions of the *subjectus* for entry without ever crossing the threshold into actual engagement with the *subjectus*. In this sense, the law is always the patrilineal transcendent force of God as produced through the petition to an outside realm of ideal and universal justice. To petition the law is to remain a supplicant, subject to the acceptance or rejection of each petition or prayer.

Three Registers of the Law

For the *subjectus*, then, it is the question of law that constitutes its mediative political function. The term "(the) law" comes from Old Norwegian and means to lay out or fix as in a partnership, layer, or stratum. It holds a sense of organization, but also a sense of distribution. In English, the term carries a tension derived from the Latin terms *lex* and *jus*, which refer to state mandated order (*lex*) and natural order (*jus*).[10] This tension is similarly reflected in the German between the terms *gesetz* (law) and *recht* (justice).

In both languages, however, the law holds three dimensions or registers important to the question of the subject and the discourse of rights. The first of these registers is the law as "a rule of conduct imposed by authority;" the second as "an agent uttering or enforcing the rules of which it consists;" and finally, the law "as implanted by nature in the human mind, or as capable of being demonstrated by reason."[11] In the first instance, as an authoritatively imposed rule of conduct, we have law as an act of control from the outside; in the second, enactive dimension, it is law as an act of enunciation on behalf of the outside. In its third register, as an inherent feature or potentiality of the mind, things become more complicated as the nature that implants the law is both inside and outside simultaneously and, as a result, holds the possibility of being comprehended outside of the regulatory construct implied by the first and second registers.

In Kafka's parable, "Before the Law," a man from the country appears before the entrance to the Law.[12] There he is met by a gatekeeper who informs him he may not enter. For many years he continues to petition the gatekeeper, and as time goes on he even petitions the fleas in the collar of the gatekeeper's greatcoat. The gatekeeper tells him among other things that even if he were to admit him there are many entrances yet to pass through, each with a gatekeeper more powerful than himself. The man from the country finally dies awaiting entrance to the Law. With his dying breath, the man asks how it happened that for all these years no others but he had begged for admittance to the Law. The gatekeeper tells him it is because this entrance was for him alone and now that he is gone it can be closed.

In this parable, the law is deployed in all three registers, often simultaneously and always as a mechanism of absolute production. For example, it is the enunciation of the gatekeeper on behalf of the law that autopoietically produces the man from the country as subservient to the deferral of his entrance to the law. This enunciation, by an intermediary of the law, produces a certain relationship—in fact a small world (inclusive of the fleas in the gatekeeper's collar) at the entrance to the law—that recycles itself in an intensive production of desire and expenditure, of infinite hope and infinite deferral. The supplicant entreats and expends in hopes of obtaining his desired end, while the mediating force defers and denies. This is, of course, the logic of the machinery of transcendent control.

Such a system of control is not premised in the law itself, but in the concept of the law. This concept of the law, never fully articulated, allows enunciation on behalf of the law without actually engaging the law itself. All directives and articulations of control are premised on the promise of a future completion of desire. Each deferral of the desire on behalf of the mediating forces pushes the threshold or actual entry further away and the resultant set of social relations shrinks, as in Kafka's parable, to a dyadic recycling of frustrated desire and supplication. Such a system is made up of an infinitude of mediations, none of which holds any actual force intrinsic to itself. Each mediation is thoroughly dependent upon the attribution of the authority of the law to itself. Such authority, however, can only be granted by the supplicant, whose desire and arrival at the gate produces the machinery itself. If the supplicant refuses the authority of the gatekeeper, the machine ceases to function and desire escapes its appropriation and exploitation by the mediative forces of the law. At such a point the law becomes obvious as the ghost in the machine; and the mediative functions, while still productive, lose their authority.

This is the terrain that Deleuze predicted when he described the control society of postmodern capitalism as a system of infinite deferral in which one never arrives.[13] There is always more training required to achieve the final job, the perfect relationship, the proper home, the better body, etc. We require less and less external discipline by the agencies of the law because the law itself, as lack and deferral, controls us. We can never arrive because we are dependent on the realm of the transcendent ideal that constantly slips away.

Immanent Law

The question remains, however, as to the nature of the law itself, beyond its juridical mediations and proliferations as a system of abstract, transcendent significations. It is here that we engage the third register of the law outlined above: the law of nature implanted in the human mind. Law without mediation, without enunciation, becomes pure production, or what Spinoza would term immanence or God (that which requires nothing other than itself in order to exist). Of course, it could be argued that God without mediation is dead. Before leaping to such rash conclusions, however, it might be worth rethinking the law as immanent production. In his lecture on Kafka, Derrida writes:

> What remains concealed and invisible in each law is thus presumably the law itself, that which makes laws of these laws, the being-law of these laws ... the law yields by withholding itself, without imparting its provenance and its site. This silence and discontinuity constitute the phenomenon of the law.[14]

If the law is the ghost in the machine, as Derrida suggests, then it is the very refusal of the law to be articulated or mediated in its actuality or fullness of being that is productive. The definitions and stories about the law cannot be the law itself. The law itself is not produced or regulated by the laws, regulations, restrictions, or enunciations which refer to it. The entrance to the law is not the law, nor are any of the enunciations of the gatekeeper the law, nor the infinite regression of gates and gatekeepers within the law. These are autopoietic productions of the law as juridical that are always exceeded by the law itself. The law's force, then, lies not in its authority or sovereign power but in its power of pure productivity. Outside of its juridical form it is not a mediated set of relations, nor a space, a diagram, a history, a story, or a concept. It produces all things and destroys all things according to its own infinitely variable logic of expression, or in another term, its own law. Again, Derrida writes:

> It seems the law as such should never give rise to any story. To be invested with its categorical authority, the law must be without history, genesis, or any possible derivation. That would be the law of the law ... Like the man from the country ... narrative accounts would try to approach the law and make it present, to enter into a relation with it, indeed to enter it and become intrinsic to it, but none of these things can be accomplished. The story of these maneuvers would merely be an account of that which escapes the story and which remains finally inaccessible to it. However, the inaccessible incites from its place of hiding.[15]

Rights and the Ontology of the *Subjectum*

To imagine that the *subjectus*, as a creature of the first two registers of the law—that is, the law as "a rule of conduct imposed by authority" and as "an agent uttering or enforcing the rules of which it consists"—can produce the conditions necessary for freedom through the juridical dispensing of rights, is to misunderstand the relations of production between the law and the subject we have outlined thus far. Put in another term, a legal positivistic ontology of human rights, which sees human rights as entitlements that the state grants or bestows upon its citizens and which, correlatively, locates rights in an infrastructure consisting of codified representations—formal declarations, legal instrumentalities, treatises, and the like—remains an ontology of mediation. In short, rights are on this positivistic view reducible to expressions of law, controlled and mediated by state forms. As Langlois has recently argued, however, "it is not these items which are human rights. Rather, these items serve to declare, protect, ensure, implement, monitor and observe human rights. They are not themselves human rights; they are one step removed."[16]

To produce rights as an actually liberatory project, it would need to be re-founded outside the juridical and the *subjectus*. It is our proposal that such a project might well be founded on the third register of the law, in the *subjectum*—that is to say, founded on non-juridical forms of law and of the subject, and produced, ultimately, within the philosophical landscape of immanence. Such a project would foreground human rights not as a form of juridical petition to the law for the permission to act, but instead as immanent potential, as absolute acts or enunciations produced and enunciated outside of modernist frameworks that privilege individual, juridical, or state forms, and produced through what Foucault has termed *relations of force* or, as Deleuze and Guattari would have it, *desire*.[17] On this immanentist view, human rights are understood as idiosyncratically produced acts of becoming, or, equally, as dialogical expressions of creative life force—that is, as embodied, corporeal powers or capacities to act in various ways that are formed and transformed in the open-ended interplay with other corporeal forces. To put it simply, human rights are created by dialogical acts in the moment of action.

This is the constitutive and creative force of subjects working together to produce new forms of the social rather than petitioning the state for the right to do so. We would argue that this is not an outside unrealized utopia but is in fact an ongoing reality that prefaces the state's appropriation of rights through the juridical. This is the refashioning of the social that occurred in the 1960s when young black men in the southern US decided to sit at a lunch counter without permission from the state or the dominant social. This is the foundation of the South African revolution when children danced in the streets and were murdered because they demanded an education. It is also, however, the less dramatic examples of cash-free and exchange-free open markets in New York city where one can simply bring and take goods as they are needed. It is the founding of dance companies throughout the world that blend people of varying neurologies and intellectual capacities against the dominant constructions of normalcy. Or the videos of alternative living that traverse the virtual world of the internet constituting by example the right to reconstitute and reshape the way one lives.

An ontological conception of human rights that highlights the constitutive significance of action and that privileges the *subjectum* over the *subjectus* diverges significantly from contemporary modernist discourses whose implicit ontologies point up the static being of human rights—their inscription in laws or juridical codes premised on jurisdictional, universal, or cosmic dispensation—rather than their processual becoming or eventness. So it is, for example, in discourses that presume that human rights are inherent in the human condition, that they inhere in humans simply in virtue of their being human. On this foundationalist view, human rights are regarded as universal, timeless essences, equally (and abstractly) possessed by all. Implicit in this conception, moreover, is the notion that human rights are metaphysically grounded in a transcendent subject, in a timeless, ahistorical, universal human nature. The subject of human rights, in this sense, is the autonomous, willing subject of modernity—a subject whose essential nature owes nothing to the social, to historicity, to eventness.

But whether we look for an ontological grounding of human rights in positive law on the one hand, or in divine or natural law on the other, human rights remain "claims to be defined in terms of possessive title ... [as] things which are owned and used like amulets to ward off [the play of] uncertainty."[18] Construed in these terms—that is, as legal entitlements or transcendent qualities—human rights may be said fundamentally to pre-exist their instantiation in action. Indeed, to speak here of the *instantiation*, or, equally, of the *expression* or *exercise* of human rights, is already to capitulate to a view that obscures the emergent, becoming, eventful quality of rights. In effect, when one is exercising, expressing, or instantiating a right, one is applying a quality one already possesses. To be sure, one may fail successfully to exercise a right—fail, for example, in one's struggles to have a right acknowledged—but even on such occasions, it is not the possession of the right itself which is at stake, for the right is what one, as a member of this particular jurisdictional community, or as a human being *tout court*, invariably and unquestionably *has*. One's success (or failure) in applying what one already possesses (in advance of any specific circumstance, as it were) is what is at issue here, not *that* one possesses it.[19] Rights, in this regard, are manifest: "they exist independently of whether they are put into effect in any one context."[20]

What this view ultimately implies is the subservience of eventness to what is generalizeable, constant, and codified (or at least potentially codifiable) in concrete, particularistic human actions. Here, the *what* or being of human rights resides not in what is specific and unrepeatable about the event, but rather in what is legally, universally, or transcendentally valid—in the rules, principles, or norms of which the individual act is a mere instantiation, or toward which it tends. In other words, the event is potentially subsumable either to a *terminus a quo*, to a point from which it proceeds or originates, or to a *terminus ad quem*, a point toward which it is proceeding. Anything situated outside the purview of origins and destinations, outside a system of transcendental and/or codified norms—any remainder or surplus not accounted for by some previously specified or potentially subsumable under a set of rules (anything unsystematizable, in short)—is deemed either inessential or inconsequential to being. But to extricate a thought, utterance, or deed from the contingency and particularity of its occurrence is precisely to transcribe away its *eventness*, that is to say, its living, unpredetermined quality, its concrete situatedness in time and place, and the particularized meaning attendant on this unsystematizable, uncodifiable specificity.[21]

An immanentist conception of human rights, in contrast, is one which foregrounds the act or event as the constitutive ground of rights. Rights are not merely instantiated but constituted, or brought forth, in action. The situated act (e.g., resistance, struggle) is not merely a means for revealing or disclosing the already given, ready-made character of a human right, but rather a means of constituting—for the first time, as it were—what that right is. In this regard, human rights are always yet-to-be-achieved, always becoming other than they are.

To claim this much about human rights, moreover, is to presuppose a particular conception of temporality: more specifically, a sense of time as open—time as becoming, as divergence, as multiplicity.[22] Constituted in open time, human rights follow many possible trajectories, paths not given in advance in some juridical code or overarching blueprint, nor in some implicit teleology. Indeed, it is this temporal openness that allows for surprisingness or eventness.[23] "For there to be eventness," writes Morson,

> there must be alternatives. Eventful events are performed in a world in which there are multiple possibilities, in which some things that could happen do not. In such a world, time ramifies and its possibilities multiply; each realized possibility opens new choices while precluding others that once could have been made. The eventful event must also be unrepeatable, that is, its meaning and weight are inextricably linked to the moment in which it is performed. Choice is *momentous*. It involves *presentness*. The same act performed later would not be quite the same act. It is therefore constituted in part by important particularities that no abstract and timeless system could foretell.[24]

Human rights qua events are the site of innovation and creativity, but also of unpredictability, of disorderly transformation, of messiness; and as such exceed the given and already-made.

To foreground the eventness of human rights is to orient us to the conditions for the *creation* of rights, which, following Deleuze, is not a matter of abstract law but rather of jurisprudence. As Deleuze puts it, "rights aren't created by codes and pronouncements but by jurisprudence. Jurisprudence is the philosophy of law, and deals with singularities [rather than particularities or instances of the general law], it advances by working out from singularities."[25] Where the law suggests restraint, limit, or restriction, jurisprudence, precisely as the temporally open *life* of law, points to eventness, deterritorialization, and—through the productivity of the concrete, individual, unrepeatable case—to the perpetual contestation and questioning of the already-given.

Capture and Release

It is our contention that state and juridical forms, particularly under regimes of late stage capitalism, take as a central defining impetus attempts to contain and turn such open-ended possibility to their own ends. More specifically, we argue that the state or juridical form appropriates productive acts, codifies these acts, and re-presents them to those who produced them as though they had always belonged to the state. In crystallizing emergent struggles into juridical categories, time is closed down. What was an open, unfinalizable process is supplanted by a finished product. Eventness is abstracted away and transcribed into a set of codes or laws. In this regard, Michel Foucault has written extensively on the:

> ways in which a supervising, regulating power needs to contain unpredictability, the eruption of the event, the emergence of singularities, and the consequent realignments of power. Indeed, it may be possible to understand his concept of power as that which functions, if not to dampen and suppress the impetus to invention and newness, then to link it as firmly and smoothly as possible to that which is already contained. Power functions to make the eruption of the event part of the fabric of the known.[26]

The centripetal, official, unifying force of codification is but one means by which the otherwise diverse and messy world of eventness is contained, and by which "the new is made recognizable and tied to the known."[27]

Contained and tied to the known—perhaps, but only ever in part. Ultimately, we think, codification is fundamentally incapable of providing a full account of the complexities of any real, singular human performance. There is always something in the concrete, historical event—a surplus, if you will—that eludes what is already given in the system of codifications and abstractions. An event is always more than an instantiation of a principle or concept or code (just as the subject is more than *subjectus*).

In order to re-claim the life force muted and/or deferred by this process of appropriation, we argue it is necessary for the subject to *ingest* the state. To ingest the state is to reverse the assimilation of the *subjectus* into the regimes of sovereignty constituted through the transcendent architecture of discipline and control. It is to refuse the parasitic process by which the state form feeds off the infinite productive moments of the acts or events of living beings and to consume, metabolize, and redistribute the sovereign force of the state into the absolute moment of the act. Specifically, we are referring to such acts of reappropriation as the water wars of Cochabamba, Peru, where Bechtel corporation was instituting a metering system for water in a region where water was a resource available for all. As resistance to the corporation increased, the central government withdrew from the area. The populace "took charge of the management of community matters during the time of the uprising. Self-defense, safety, food distribution in the city, were all in the hands of the people who organized themselves without any help from the state or its representatives."[28] This is to assert the full material force of the *subjectum* through the rite of sacrament by which God (or the sovereign outside) is made flesh (or instantiated as fully material) so as to be destroyed and consumed so that the outside can be made a fully expressive force in each of those who ingest it. The act of ingesting the state is one of collapsing sovereign force into its own expressive capacities.

In another term, this is the moment in which the subject refuses sovereignty as a transcendent outside. Instead, rule is taken within the collective force of life as a thoroughly material force. That is to say that rule becomes a question of what is done as a series of constitutive acts that arise immanently and autopoetically, as Marx would have it, from those acting and creating. In a contemporary example, this is the refusal of psychiatry and the mental health services of the state by those labeled schizophrenic and the reconstitution of those services as something creatively produced together by these subjects and their allies as the Hearing Voices Network or the advocates for neurological diversity.[29] In each of these instances the subjects wrest the sovereignty of state rule and transform it into creative assemblages of living creative activity that produce new forms of care and the right to be cared for through self rule.

The Multitude

We argue, accordingly, that rights *qua* rights neither require nor depend on the ability to petition the state for legal status, but rather are produced within the forms of daily life of what Hardt and Negri and others have termed the *multitude*.[30] This multitude, in our terms, is produced through the effects of globalization as a network of idiosyncratic creative forces comprising all acts of production. Within this framework every action produces the possibility of further action; every action gives rise, in other words, to an inappropriable, untranscribable, uncodifiable as-yetness, to a field of infinite possibility.

Historically, the category of the multitude, or the many, has been positioned contrastively against the much more well-known category of the people, or the one. In seventeenth-century theoretical-philosophical debates over the nature of collective experience, it was the Hobbesian notion of the people that prevailed—the Spinozist multitude emerging in these ideological clashes as "the losing term, the concept which got the worst of it."[31] For Hobbes, the possibility of collective action required a political oneness as its enabling foundation—a singularity of will and purpose, a centripetal, homogenizing swirl that gathered within its vortex the disparate plurality of the many, of the multitude. Inherent in the state of nature, the multitude was an undomesticated form of the many, preceding and antithetical to a political mode of being. As Virno notes, this multitude "shuns political unity, resists authority, does not enter into lasting agreements, never attains the *status* of a juridical person because it never transfers its own natural rights to the sovereign."[32] As such, the multitude was, for Hobbes at least, incapable of existing alongside the people—more than that, it was a threat in whose unchecked potentials lay the ever-present threat of civil war. In this was also the threat of anarchy and, indeed, a system such as Virno describes holds a semblance to anarchy in its call for a refusal of sovereign rule. However, in their writings on the multitude, Hardt and Negri emphasize the multitude not as an anarchic system of no rule but a distributive system of self rule premised in the becoming common of multiplicity.

In contrast to Hobbes, Spinoza defended the primacy of centrifugal, dispersive forces over centripetal, unifying tendencies. For Spinoza, the multitude (*multitudo*) captured the inescapable, ineradicable persistence of the many, of plurality, in forms of collective-associative life. Spinoza proposed a dystopic politics of struggle and collision in which the infinite capacities of God (which he referred to as substance) as creative expression produced the world through the striving of all to persist in unmediated idiosyncratic variation. However, this was not civil war as Hobbes would have it or the war of all against all, but rather the development of political force with a new form of rule or sovereignty premised on the deployment of radical idiosyncratic difference in the service of common political projects. Such a political entity he termed the multitude. Hardt and Negri, following Spinoza, remark:

> The multitude designates an active social subject, which acts on the basis of what the singularities share in common. The multitude is an internally different, multiple social subject whose constitution and action is based not on identity or unity ... but on what it has in common.[33]

There are two critical elements of importance in this description of the multitude. The first is the distinction of a social subject radically different from the *subjectus* of juridical social forms. This is subjectivity, not subjected to, but produced from and expressive of the capacities of sovereignty as political force. In this, the concept of the one differs significantly from the concept of the one as the people in Hobbes. In Hobbes, the one must be produced through a transcendent political will, an appeal to an ideal political form of governance modeled on a dominating, disciplinary, and patriarchal God. Freedom as granted from the father, even in the form of natural right or democratic impetus, must be directed and controlled so as to not exceed the capacity for sovereign discipline.

> Every Sovereign power ... necessarily forms a political body of which there is a head that commands, limbs that obey, and organs that function together to support the ruler. The concept of the multitude challenges this accepted truth of sovereignty ... rather than a political body with one that commands and others that obey, the multitude is living flesh that rules itself.[34]

In Spinoza, political force is derived from God as substance or that which simply produces all. In this, the political social subjectivity of the multitude is not a *subjectus* which must be ruled from above, but the idiosyncratic expressions of substance or God that are divinely ordained to persist as aspects of God's productive capacity. The social body, then, is not one ruled by the head, but rather a body that rules itself through what it shares in common. Such a body, to continue the analogy, does not function by the head ordering the lungs to breathe, the heart to beat, or the hands to raise up, but rather through the mutual interactions of an infinitely complex exchange of idiosyncratic cellular and electrical impulses operating in common as an assemblage of bodies producing the living being in its capacity to persist over time.

To return to the issue of rights, the multitude as a social subjectivity constitutes a political body for whom an appeal to a transcendent power holds no use. The liver need not petition the brain to function. Its function is an interaction with all of the elements of the body simultaneously which requires an ongoing calibration of all components of the system in ongoing struggle and collision in order to survive. Rights, in this idiom, are produced in cooperative exchange and struggle in the moment of the actions of singularities in collision. While the brain may recognize some small portion of this process through its conscious function, it simply never has sufficient information to adequately rule or dispense the right to do anything. We would argue the same holds true for any transcendent form of sovereignty, such as the nation state, or even new forms of sovereignty, such as the form of global capital that Hardt and Negri have termed *empire*.[35]

For Bakhtin, too, the unofficial centrifugal forces of language and culture forever unsettle (disrupt) the unifying order imposed by official, centripetal cultural forces, such as law, the juridical, and the sovereign. Bakhtin uses the term *heteroglossia* to refer to the dynamic, linguistic-ideological diversity present in both art and life.[36] The term implies that both societies on the one hand, and individuals on the other, are not unified, monolithic entities, but rather the sites of linguistic and social diversity, characterized by an intense struggle among coexisting voices and their corresponding views of the world. This multivoicedness, accordingly, problematizes any unity that may be posited in cultural life. What the presence of such forces suggests is that unity in language or in any other cultural entity is not something given in advance, not something originary and fundamental, but rather something posited—through force or consent. Unity, however imposed or established, is always provisional and incomplete, "always opposed to the essential messiness of the world."[37]

Rights, we argue, are produced precisely through the messy actions and interactions of singular and idiosyncratic social subjects. Such acts proliferate across the social in a dizzying array of variation and extension. Such a heteronymous, indeterminate, promiscuous, and fecund set of infinite combination is not without its own logic of force and direction. Indeed, for us, the political project of an immanent right of the multitude is far from an anarchic absence of rule. Indeed, as Hardt and Negri point out, there is a rule of the multitude, but such rule arises not from a hierarchical sovereignty but from the productions of the broadest array of social interchanges and exchanges.[38] Of course this broad array can only be found in the largest assemblages of life, not necessarily in the denumerable sense, but rather in the sense of particularized assemblages of bodies without number, that is, from the bottom up.

As we have tried to make clear, rights as instantiated act, free from petition to the sovereignty of law of the state, is not an absence of law. Instead, it is an assertion of the laws of production itself and as such operates along the event horizon of every historical moment. Rights as acts are always derived out of the historical tendencies of a given moment of social production.[39] They are always a thoroughly material ontological instantiation. In this, moreover, we are not advocating becoming as a potential ontological moment to come; nor becoming of a particular being *thing*. Rather, we are proposing that rights become in the moment of their enactment by living social beings as full ontological expressions of life erupting against the dead edifice of sovereign domination and the type of disciplinary law that would attempt to constrain the fecundity of living force.

We are not, however, arguing that there is no place for discipline. In fact, every act constitutes a disciplinary moment in which all other possible actions have been excluded from the moment of its enactment. Rights in this sense are final. Once they have been produced within the social through the act—once they *be*—they cannot be undone. They can be avoided, hidden, constrained, disciplined to other ends, legislated, and even dominated for periods of time, but acts, once enacted, reverberate throughout the social forever as that which can now be done. Further, such acts open the door to all other acts of like kind that have not yet been. It is this we mean by the infinite potential of rights—those acts which open the force of creative expression as the final actions of political will.

This is the right of the multitude that erupts across history in act after act of ontological force. It is not force as the capacity to produce stratifications and divisions between bodies or subjects. Such an assertion of right is the province of the state and its law. Rather it is the immanent force of self production as an ontological capacity of becoming that will not be denied. Such rights are premised in the infinitude of life's virtual surplus of that which has not yet been. In the face of the rather overwhelming sovereign force of global capitalism, in which all aspects of the social are turned to the logic of the market, rights as acts refuse the semiotic in favor of the instantiation of the actual. Such moments of insurrection are endemic across the globe, and no system of domination has ever been able to halt or even successfully control their proliferation. Rights in this sense are the weeds in the garden of the state. Even the smallest crack opens a new site for their production.

Notes

[1] The Doors, "The Soft Parade" (Elektra Records, 1969).
[2] Michael Hardt and Antonio Negri, *Empire* (Cambridge, MA: Harvard University Press, 2000).
[3] We leave aside the question of the postmodern subject as delineated in Deleuze's essay on "control societies" as a variation of discipline that exceeds the juridical and the discourse on rights related to law which we are engaging in this essay. See Gilles Deleuze, *Negotiations 1972–1990*, trans. Martin Joughin (New York: Columbia University Press, 1995).
[4] Étienne Balibar, "Citizen Subject," in *Who Comes After the Subject?*, ed. Eduardo Cadava, Peter Connor, and Jean-Luc Nancy (New York: Routledge, 1991), 38, emphasis in original.
[5] Étienne Balibar, "Subjection and Subjectivation," in *Supposing the Subject*, ed. Joan Copjec (London: Verso, 1994), 8; emphasis in original.
[6] Mikhail Bakhtin, *Problems of Dostoevsky's Poetics*, trans. Caryl Emerson (Minneapolis, MN: University of Minnesota Press, 1984), 188.
[7] Slavoj Žižek, *The Sublime Object of Ideology* (London: Verso, 1989), 122.
[8] Michael Hardt and Antonio Negri, *Multitude: War and Democracy in the Age of Empire* (New York: Penguin, 2004).
[9] Niklas Luhmann, *Social Systems*, trans. John Bednarz, Jr. (Stanford, CA: Stanford University Press, 1995).
[10] *OED Online*, s.v. "Law," http://dictionary.oed.com (accessed January 16, 2009).
[11] Ibid.
[12] Franz Kafka, *The Penal Colony: Stories and Short Pieces*, trans. Willa Muir and Edwin Muir (New York: Schocken, 1976).
[13] Deleuze, *Negotiations 1972–1990*.

[14] Jacques Derrida, "Before the Law," in *Acts of Literature*, ed. Derek Attridge (London: Routledge, 1992), 192.
[15] Ibid.
[16] Anthony J. Langlois, "The Elusive Ontology of Human Rights," *Global Society* 18 (2004): 244.
[17] Michel Foucault, *The History of Sexuality, Vol. 1: An Introduction*, trans. Robert Hurley (New York: Vintage, 1990); Gilles Deleuze and Felix Guattari, *A Thousand Plateaus: Capitalism and Schizophrenia*, trans. Brian Massumi (Minneapolis: University of Minnesota Press, 1987).
[18] Robin Holt, *Wittgenstein, Politics, and Human Rights* (New York: Routledge, 1997), 3.
[19] See Dieter Misgeld and David W. Jardine, "Hermeneutics as the Undisciplined Child: Hermeneutics and Technical Images of Education,' in *Entering the Circle: Hermeneutic Investigation in Psychology*, ed. Martin. J. Packer and Richard B. Addison (Albany: State University of New York Press, 1989).
[20] Holt, *Wittgenstein, Politics, and Human Rights*, 4.
[21] Mikhail Bakhtin, *Toward a Philosophy of the Act*, trans. Vadim Liapunov (Austin, TX: University of Texas Press, 1993).
[22] Elizabeth Grosz, "Thinking the New: Of Futures Yet Unthought," in *Becomings: Explorations in Time, Memory, and Futures*, trans. Elizabeth Grosz (Ithaca, NY: Cornell University Press, 1999).
[23] Bakhtin, *Toward a Philosophy of the Act*.
[24] Gary Saul Morson, *Narrative and Freedom: The Shadows of Time* (New Haven, CT: Yale University Press, 1994), 22; emphasis in original.
[25] Deleuze, *Negotiations 1972–1990*, 153.
[26] Grosz, "Thinking the New: Of Futures Yet Unthought," 16.
[27] Ibid.
[28] Claudia Lopez, "Cochabamba's Water Wars: The Start of Other Struggles," *Upside Down World*, http://upsidedownworld.org/main/bolivia-archives-31/300-cochabambas-water-war-the-start-of-other-struggles (accessed May 19, 2010).
[29] See Hearing Voices Network (http://www.hearing-voices.org/) and Neurodiversity (http://www.neurodiversity.com/main.html). The Hearing Voices Network (HVN) emerged as an alternative to traditional psychiatric approaches which consider voice hearing simply as form of auditory hallucination. The HVN aims to raise awareness of this phenomenon, offering other explanations for voice hearing (e.g., extreme stress or trauma) and providing help, support, and understanding to people who experience hearing voices. Neurodiversity is a self-advocacy movement which asserts that non-normative (neurodivergent) neurological development is simply difference that should be acknowledged and respected on its own terms.
[30] Hardt and Negri, *Multitude: War and Democracy in the Age of Empire*.
[31] Paolo Virno, *A Grammar of the Multitude*, trans. Isabella Bertoletti, James Cascaito, and Andrea Casson (Los Angeles: Semiotext[e], 2004), 21.
[32] Ibid., 23.
[33] Hardt and Negri, *Multitude: War and Democracy in the Age of Empire*, 100.
[34] Ibid.
[35] Hardt and Negri, *Empire*.
[36] Mikhail Bakhtin, *The Dialogic Imagination*, trans. Caryl Emerson and Michael Holquist (Austin, TX: University of Texas Press, 1981), 270.
[37] Gary Saul Morson and Caryl Emerson, *Mikhail Bakhtin: Creation of a Prosaics* (Stanford, CA: Stanford University Press, 1990), 139.
[38] Hardt and Negri, *Multitude: War and Democracy in the Age of Empire*.
[39] Ibid.

Human Rights and an Ethic of truths: Pragmatic Dilemmas and Discursive Interventions[1]

Leonard C. Hawes

This paper begins with a critique of the concept of "rights" as that term is discursively deployed in the service of conventional human rights interventions. Four aporias of human rights discourse are foregrounded and serve as the basis on which six posthumanist claims are advanced. These claims are made to reimagine the concept of "rights" and rights-based discourse along the philosophical pathways mapped by Alain Badiou. Those pathways lead to spaces where the global and the local can be rethought as, in large measure, scale invariant; substantively, the local and the global differ dramatically; processually, the positions along the arc articulating substance to process function as immanent analogues. Multicultural immigration circumstances in Copenhagen preceding the "cartoon controversies" are discussed in discursive terms more or less unrelated to the discursive figures of "human rights," demonstrating the possibility of realizing immanent human rights objectives without resorting to transcendent human rights discourse.

Aporias of Human Rights Discourse

One of the many ironies of human rights-based discourse is that by formulating political demands as rights, the better to secure the legitimacy of those demands in political negotiations, what frequently happens is that the issues at stake become non-negotiable.[2] Rights-based claims are supposed to function as trumps, as rhetorically self-evident truths and transcendent positions that stand above and beyond contestation. The operative, if usually implicit, assumption is that if certain human rights are subscribed to universally, appeals to those rights in the "event" of their violation will somehow set aright the aggrieved conditions and elevate the human status of the victims. If attention is called to abuses of human rights, then political, legal, and humanitarian action can be brought to bear on such egregious circumstances, and the condition of the entire species thereby can be elevated. Unnecessary suffering can be done away with, at least in some small measure.

Instead of resolving disputes, however, rights-based arguments more often than not escalate antagonisms by claiming the unassailable moral high ground. The claim of such arguments is construed as an indisputable right. Rights discourse has the potential to create a common framework of talking points capable of facilitating dialogue and deliberation; nonetheless to claim a right is not, *ipso facto*, to occupy some privileged and transcendent position. A common discourse does not necessarily facilitate processes leading to agreements; to the contrary, expectations that prior agreements regarding abstracted rights will be universally honored actually complicate resolution processes.

Invoking a right or some set of rights often solidifies positions, raises stakes, and escalates intensities by abstracting positions from lived experience, moralizing conditions in ways that render them inviolable and nonnegotiable, leaving open only the options of righteous litigation and pietistic war. Ignatieff concurs, acknowledging that "it is an illusion to suppose that the function of human rights is to define a higher realm of shared moral values that will assist in finding common ground."[3] Discourses shift from praxiological considerations, i.e., from negotiating and mediating immanent conditions and circumstances, to ontological considerations, i.e., to debating the transcendent nature of ethics and the "right" to be honored, often without much consideration of the "obligations" that attend those "rights."

Consider Mark Tushnet's incisive critique of the paradoxes inherent to the concept of "rights," which is as pertinent to the human rights debate today (albeit in several different respects) as it was in the mid-1980s.[4] Tushnet frames his critique of "rights" as a Schumpeterian act of creative destruction, an act of destroying the coherence and the sense of a concept—in this case, the concept of "rights"—in order to produce possibilities for the creation of progressive social action. He advances four carefully articulated arguments. The first of these arguments is that *rights are inherently unstable*. Small changes in social circumstances and cultural conditions shift the parameters of inequity, injustice, and oppression, and thereby change the ways in which rights violations are framed so as to be as poignant as possible.

The second argument is that *rights are indeterminate*. Claiming a right in the face of its violation most often produces a counter-claim in some form, but rarely does claiming a right produce the changes necessary to eradicate the violation and establish or restore the right in question. The third argument is that, once claimed, *any particular right converts ultimately into empty abstractions*. Making claims to rights necessarily reifies lived experience, abstracting it as a transcendent category. And finally, *invoking rights actually impedes progressive social forces*. Invoking rights rigidifies positions by increasing the gravity (i.e., the density and intensity) of a claim, escalating the intensities of the differences between the claimed positions, making negotiation, mediation, and dialogue more difficult, if not impossible.

Consider each in turn. Animating the claim that any particular right is inherently unstable is the presupposition that the concept of rights is productively invoked only when some *specific* right is asserted in some *specific* set of circumstances.[5] Inequities and infringements provide justificatory grounds for invoking the concept of a right, which (by right and entitlement) it is presupposed, *ought* to be recognized and acknowledged as a right, hence the deontological, moral force of the claim. In other words, a justification for a need to be satisfied is to frame a need as a right. What is scarce or absent becomes a need insofar as an inequity or an infringement is recognized. It is recognized and acknowledged as a need for that to which a body is entitled, has a right, and currently lacks.

The concept of human rights presupposes that humans are somehow superior to other forms of life, and that they are thereby privileged and deserving of having certain fundamental, existential conditions guaranteed. Not to do everything possible to honor that guarantee is to be inhuman(e). Human rights, however, are routinely violated according to one set of standards or another insofar as they can never be universally guaranteed across qualitatively different sociocultural formations. Moralistic pleas for human rights to be honored notwithstanding, such pleading in and of itself seems to have very little material effect. One important difficulty obvious enough in hindsight is that small changes in sociocultural conditions of necessity alter the configuration of any conflict assemblage, which in turn alters the forms and sites of inequity and infringement. Whether any particular right is being violated depends upon which contingent conditions change; and this fact invalidates any claim of universality for rights. Rights are of necessity contingent, not universal. The pivotal question is who gets to name and claim what human rights are, when and how they are violated, who violates them, and what is to be done.

It is usually much more effective in any number of ways to address the libidinal singularities of the immanent conditions of alleged infringements and inequities (without overlooking the rational generalities) than it is to discursively transcend immanent conditions by means of abstracting libidinal forces to produce rational universal categories stripped bare of lived experience. The concept of universal human rights becomes naively irrelevant at best and cynically counterproductive at worst from the position of an embodied subject (on whatever scale of analysis such a body is defined). A response to inequity and infringement designed for a singular set of circumstances promises to be better fitted to immanent political, economic, cultural, religious, and aesthetic conditions than does a response consisting in the discursive invocation of and reliance on abstracted categories of a transcendent set of universal principles.

The recognition and invocation of a specific right, then, depends upon the immanent conditions of a singular sociocultural formation. Every specific right is contingent on specific social and technological facts and their operations. A set of rights recognized and acknowledged at a particular moment is co-extensive with the constitution of its sociocultural formation at that moment. The conditions of a cultural formation's social structures define exactly what kind of discursive and non-discursive practices have pragmatic traction and make practical, tactical, and strategic sense in a particular set of circumstances. Rights-based discourse, then, can make sense of only and exactly these singular conditions and circumstances at a particular moment. In brief, rights-based discourse cannot be linked to specifiable results without stipulating so many details about the sociocultural context of the alleged rights violations as to transform rights claims into detailed critical descriptions of entire cultures and their social institutions.

In this respect, the fundamental indeterminacy of rights is a corollary of the inherent instability of rights. Rights do not and cannot exist in isolation. Each rights-based claim fits into a background of other rights-based claims that can be used to define the limits of any particular right drawn into any particular controversy. Negotiating rights and deciding which to background and which to foreground requires three determinations. The first of these involves determining the unit of measurement for the values at stake and how to actually measure the values affected when particular rights stand in need of balancing. How are the relative gravities and intensities of the disputed rights to be measured? The second determination specifies the necessary consequences of negotiating any right or set of rights. How are the consequences of the alleged rights violations to be measured against the rights that would be violated if the alleged rights violations were to be remedied? Finally, the necessary level of generality at which the first two considerations are to be determined must be stipulated. At what level of detail and specificity is the discourse to be cast in order to make these determinations? The conundrum is that rights-based conflicts remain coherent only so long as conflicting factions agree not to question these three determinations. As soon as the *implicit measure of value*, the *level of discursive generality*, or the *description of context* is questioned, the coherence of a rights-based argument begins to dissolve.

Returning to Tushnet's reification critique, rights-based discourse captures the contradictory predicament of people as at once alone and together, independent and in solidarity.[6] Independence and solidarity are not so much instances of abstract rights as they are experiences that are eviscerated as soon as they are characterized as abstract rights. Reification desiccates the intensities, textures, and forces of lived experience by abstracting them as concepts. The effect is that rights-based discourse takes as its goal the abstraction of rights from lived experience thereby transcending lived experience rather than actualizing political strategies and tactics based on the singular and actual experience of solidarity and individuality. Tushnet contends that if we treat experiences of solidarity and individuality as directly relevant to political discussions (instead of coding brutality and violence in the language of rights), we better address political issues ethically on immanent planes of analysis, tactic, strategy, and action.

Finally, the discourse of rights is vulnerable in terms of its political disutility.[7] Rights discourse not only does not do much good, it actually does harm. Tushnet claims that, in mainstream Western culture, the image of negative and reactive rights (and thus their associated philosophies) overshadows positive and affirmative rights and philosophies, and may in fact obstruct them. Rights discourse is meaningful only when placed within its full legal and social context.[8] After reviewing Habermas's work on universal human interests and the ideal speech situation, and then sharing his grave reservations about the idealism of that work, Tushnet moves to a position he calls "oppositionism." The rationale for "oppositionism" rests on three *a priori* conditions.

First, there is unnecessary suffering in the world, and we have chosen to create and maintain systems that promote such unnecessary suffering. Second, this fact alone justifies our opposition to the way things are. And third, there are no grand strategies for general transformation, only careful analyses of existing, localized circumstances. Social worlds dissolve into multiplicities of choices. Nothing is necessary. Everything is contingent. And one need not be resigned to how things are. Things can be otherwise.[9] Tushnet derives six claims from these *a priori* conditions that support his decision to adopt the critical practices of "Oppositionism".

Rethinking Human Rights Discourse

I rehearse Tushnet's six claims here to both frame and introduce a way of reimagining the concept of rights and of rights-based discourse, along with some of the ways rights-based discourse works in agonistic and antagonistic conflicts. Here are those claims: (1) the social world dissolves into a set of choices one has made; (2) every decision becomes political; (3) nothing is necessary; (4) everything is contingent; (5) I need not resign myself to how things are; and (6) things can be otherwise. Suffering is uneven and ubiquitous; oppressive relations of governance and abusive relationships of daily life are responsible for much of this suffering; these relations and relationships are in some measure the interdependent products of human choices; and the worlds that these oppressive relations and relationships constitute are contingent worlds of conflicting and contesting discourses.

Mine is the illiberal, post-humanist task of critiquing several of the pivotal presumptions of human rights discourse by addressing the instability, indeterminacy, abstractness, and disutility of the very idea of human rights, and to assess the consequences of deploying rights-based discourse in the name of its identified victims. My primary objective in doing so is to engage inevitably contingent and immanent conflict with discursive practices that reframe and resolve antagonistic conflicts along more agonistic lines. Discursive practices that map nomadic-libidinal trajectories of desiring-production may engage conflict currently framed as human rights violations more inventively and productively than do conventional discursive practices that claim and occupy sedentary-rational (i.e., legal) positions of rights and entitlements. At question is whether discursive practices that deploy rights-based claims and counter-claims are politically, intellectually, and ethically productive.

The questions to be addressed have to do with how a critique of rights-based discourses can inform negotiating, mediating, and dialoguing in ways that generate potentiality and possibility. Vigorous agonistic and antagonistic conflict is seldom engaged in and mediated as an initial response to critical differences. First responses following the shock and awe of an event more often are antagonistic retaliations and reluctant bargaining (e.g., the "event" we refer to as 9/11). The counter-intuitive move is to engage agonistic conflicts passionately and to negotiate the double binds and death spirals of antagonistic conflicts early on, even prematurely, before the desiring-production of revenge, violence, and blood-lust become self-producing, autopoietic systems. When conflict escalates from agonistics to antagonistics, one or more factions of the escalating conflict inevitably claim certain rights, defend particular identities, and assert specific truths.

Rights are transcendent insofar as they define the universal interests of the powerless. The powerful take care of *their/our own* rights. To the extent that the foundations of universal interests are unevenly and variously moralistic, the idea of universal rights presupposes the reasoned and reasonable actions and commitments of others, and of course, the willingness of others to submit conflicts to some form of adjudication. The founding moral commitment of rights discourse is to enlightened, reasoned, and reasonable deliberation. Insofar as we are not willing to agree about what a minimal human rights regime should include, the best way to proceed is via rational discourse and reasonable debate. But that sets up the paradoxical injunction to "tolerate unreasonable people" ("unreasonable" is determined, of course, by our standards of "reasonableness," not theirs) even when it is unreasonable to do so (again, "unreasonable" is determined by our standards of rationality, not theirs), as long as they do not threaten to harm us or others (again, same caveat).

It is our claim, of course, not theirs (whichever particular them is resisting our claims at any particular moment) that human rights generally and collectively are universal and should be adhered to. But what happens if and when unreasonable people (as determined by us, i.e., those of us controlling, ultimately, the monopoly on violence) are not tolerated, which of course they are not much of the time? Who gets to make the determination of what constitutes a threat of harm to others and a violation of their rights? Which particular others make such determinations? And how are those determinations made? Keep in mind that the proliferation of human rights beyond some minimally necessary set of rights to protect persons as purposive agents (whatever that minimal set might be) actually weakens rather than strengthens the resolve of the potential enforcers of and adherents to those rights.

It is beyond the scope of this paper to rehearse the history of the debates over universal human rights, debates that escalated in the US over slavery and its abolition and that continued throughout the Civil War, resumed after the Second World War in the aftermath of the Holocaust, and provided the moral impetus for the Civil Rights Movement. These ongoing debates have produced what Michael Ignatieff[10] calls "the juridical revolution" in human rights advocacy, a "revolution" whose form and content since 1945 produced the Universal Declaration of Human Rights and the Geneva Conventions of 1948, the revision of the Geneva Conventions of 1949, and the International Convention on Asylum of 1951.

Ignatieff argues that the purpose of the human rights movement is to protect human agency, which is accomplished by protecting human agents from abuse and oppression. Human rights, conceptualized as political instruments rather than as shrines of humanistic secular worship (Ignatieff's figure for conventional thinking about human rights), protect a core of negative freedoms. In her introduction to Ignatieff's essays, Amy Gutmann maintains that human agency supports more than negative freedom and liberty—i.e., freedom *from* torture, abuse, cruelty, oppression, degradation, and the like—by arguing *for* positive freedoms and liberties. The right *to* subsistence, she contends, is as necessary for human agency as is the right *against* torture, abuse, and cruelty. If protections against cruelty and degradation—i.e., freedom *from* harm and freedom *to* live a (decent) life—are not human rights, she argues, then perhaps nothing is.[11]

For Ignatieff, agency is the core value animating human rights. Without human rights, people lack agency. Gutmann claims that although agency is crucial for human rights, a human rights regime is most likely to win widespread, even if not universal, consent if it is based on multiple foundations. A philosophical foundation, to function as a foundation, needs to be so good as to be transparent, self-evident, indisputable, and unassailable; in short, to be hegemonic. Ignatieff's founding principle, that humans are purposive and self-originating agents of rights-based claims, is far from having won universal consent. It certainly flies in the face of much of the post-humanist project, most pointedly Alain Badiou's work on an ethic of truths and the production of evil, which is taken up in the next section.

The assumption of self-originating agency is becoming increasingly problematic and controversial in theory, politics, and the quotidian relations and relationships that constitute families, institutions, regions, and nation-states. To his credit, Ignatieff wants to avoid foundational arguments over claims of human dignity, natural law, and divine creative purpose. Instead, he argues, a universal regime of human rights should be compatible with moral pluralism. Guttman argues that plural foundations would make a human rights regime more broadly acceptable to heterogeneous cultural formations, and that, insofar as a human rights regime is conceived as a political instrument, human agency, dignity, and equality are three pillars of the foundations that are not necessarily mutually exclusive.

Moral pluralism does not hold sway however, as is evidenced by the necessity of phrasing human rights as declarations of what *should be* the case, what *ought to be* put in place, what we *have to do*, and what *must be done*. Human rights are identified relative to the harm their absence creates, i.e. as conditions that currently do not exist, but should "by right." Pleas for the recognition of rights give rise to the argument that a universal regime of human rights and moral pluralism *ought to be* compatible. But quite obviously they are not. Those pleas would not be necessary if moral pluralism and universal human rights were, in fact, articulated. The question is how best to transform what *is* into what *should be*.

Although Ignatieff[12] judiciously avoids the seemingly endless debates about human dignity, natural law, and divine creative purpose, that still leaves him in search of a plane of transcendence on which to mount his claims of universality, humanity, and rights. The problem of foundationalism, along with its commitment to universalism, is that a moral argument—whether it is formulated as a moral singularity or a moral plurality, and whether that morality is elaborated as a thin or thick moral philosophy—sidesteps the more subtle ethical questions that an invocation of human rights poses but does not address.

Consider nationalism as a narrative articulation of collective agency and self-determination. Nationalism is claimed as a human right on behalf of a self-determining subject (i.e., a "people"). But nationalism, in actual historical practice, is a response to one set of human rights problems and the creation of another. Arnold Mindell contrasts nationalism to class. Nationalism is based on the assumption that the fundamental cleavage in society divides people vertically into ethno-national groups. Class, on the other hand, divides a people horizontally, on the assumption that class lines intersect and cut across national lines.[13] Those intersections of horizontal "classist" lines and vertical "nationalist" lines are not only sites of intense conflicts, but their cross-currents render consensus on a universal human rights regime impossible.

Nation-states assume the authority to oppress, abuse, marginalize, and trivialize subjects in the name of the rights of the nation-state's sovereign self-determination. In fact, whenever collective self-determination is conflated with national sovereignty, the risk of other rights violations being committed increases, at times in ways that support such violations in the name of national sovereignty.

Human Rights Discourse and Alain Badiou

I contend that Badiou's ontological work is one line of thinking that enables us to rethink and perhaps reformulate human rights discourse. Badiou contends that contemporary human rights theory and practice amount to little else than the selective tolerance of difference. Rather than merely asking for and then demanding the universal respect of negative human rights (i.e., rights to be protected from certain threats and dangers), Badiou argues for the affirmation of the unique, "evental" truths of life itself. Much of his critique of what he refers to as the ethical ideology of the Other is embedded in his more encompassing critique of consensus thinking regarding the discourse of (universal) human rights. Negative human rights discourse amounts to a generally universal imposition and application of the Truth of particular and special interests. Positive human rights, on the other hand, amounts to affirming the "evental" truths of partisan, singular, and absolutely distinct universality.

An ethic of truths recognizes and affirms the immortal value of partisan and singular truths (in the sense that "evental" truth is experienced as exceeding any one mortal life). An ethical ideology of the Other holds to the Truth of universal human rights coupled with a more or less patronizing tolerance of differences within a presupposed ontological One, or Same, or Unity of merely mortal privileges. Human rights advocacy presupposes the right and the power to identify whose rights are being violated and what should be done about it. Once identified, it becomes difficult if not impossible for victims of human rights violations to escape their subject positions of subordination. A human rights body is guaranteed the dominant subject position. The presumption of superiority is determined in the act of stipulating who gets to identify the victims and who gets to determine what constitutes aid, assistance, enlightenment, and in some instances salvation.

Any difference or set of differences is framed in ways that privilege dominant bodies at the expense of subordinated bodies, and those relations are normalized hegemonically, as just the way things are. For Badiou, truths of partisan, singular, and unique universality however, hold to the possibility of the emergence of the Same-which-is-not-yet. It is the "which-is-not-yet" portion of that phrase that is important to understand. Both Badiou and Deleuze rely on Nietzsche's figure of "The Throw of the Dice" to account for Chance in the emergence of truth. But each understands Nietzsche's figure for the principle of eternal return differently. According to Badiou, Deleuze thinks Chance is singular, as probability theory presupposes Chance to be One, ultimately unitary. Indefinite throws of the dice (assuming they are not loaded) ultimately produce the Same randomness—equiprobability—for Deleuze, the eternal return of "... *the original throw of the dice with the power of affirming chance.*"[14] Badiou, on the other hand, thinks of Chance as plural, i.e., "it is by chance that a particular chance happens."[15] The contingent and fortuitous events from which singular and incomparable truths originate must be multiple and separated by a void, not ultimately from a One, or the Same; hence for Badiou, chance is plural. The Same is always already that "which-is-not-yet."

According to Badiou, betraying a singular and incomparable truth by giving it up or giving up on it, mistaking it for its resemblances, and/or imposing it as *the* Truth by forcing it universally as One and the Same on Others constitutes Evil. As such, Evil is not the original condition of the world that an ethical ideology of Other is supposed to countermand. Rather, Evil is produced from efforts to do Good to/for/on Others. I contend that the practical and ontological implications of this reversal of thinking are as promising as they are counterintuitive. At sites of "events" situated vulnerably at the edges of a void, breaking the categories of approved ordinary knowledge and thereby evading commonsensical classifications, there is no "ethics in general" or "general ethics," and no generally transcendent principles of human rights. What is singularly universal is immanence; what is universally general is formulated subsequently as transcendence. Transcending immanence in search of universally general categories, particularly when motivated by the best of intensions, constitutes Evil by propounding a transcendent Truth to be imposed on innumerable singular, immanent truth conditions.[16]

Consider the ideological pillars of the ethics of universal (i.e., transcendent) human rights. According to Badiou, these pillars consist in four presuppositions: (1) there is a general human subject who is passive, pathetic, and reflexive (i.e., a subject who suffers, a victim), yet that subject is also assumed to be an active self-determining subject capable of making accountable judgments; (2) politics is subordinated to ethics; it is the sympathetic, compassionate and indignant judgment of the superior, privileged spectator that matters most; (3) Evil is that from which Good is derived, not the other way about; and (4) human rights are rights to non-Evil, rights to not be offended or mistreated with respect to one's life, one's body, or one's cultural identity.[17]

In short, these are the tenets of an ethic of (transcendent) human rights, which in their very formulation constitute some humans as victims and some as rescuers. Victims stand in need of (our) assistance, support, aid, rescue, if not enlightenment and salvation. The rescuing is to be provided by humans who not only are not victims, but are in fact rescuers, humanitarians, and saviors. It is in our best interest as privileged rescuers to identify victims; it is our *raison d'être* as rescuers. It is the very foundation of (our) superiority. Humans, it is supposed, are victims insofar as they live in conditions of extreme scarcity in a world of scarce resources, except for all but a privileged minority, i.e., us. Ironically, invoking the prevailing conventional ethical principles in an effort to counteract human rights abuses brought on by scarcity actually reinforces and reinscribes the validity of the ideology of the rescuer/victim dialectic that bars identified victims from acquiring the agency of self-determination.

Such an ethics framed as negative human rights is also incapable of sustaining carefully situated and decisive political and discursive interventions. Rescuers rarely implicate and index themselves in the system of scarcity for most and excess for few. How are the interventions of rescuers complicit in the productions and reproductions of the scarcity conditions that disadvantage the "victims" in the first place? An ethic of Other lacks a coherent conception of Evil. Insatiable needs in a system of presupposed scarcity become rights that can never be met, much less guaranteed. Ironically, then, Evil is produced by means of imposing a transcendent, universal Truth (of law, economics, governance, religion, and so forth) on immanent, singular conditions of inequality and injustice in an effort to do Good. Moral discomfort is addressed and consciences are salved, but conditions of oppression and dependency are recreated in the very process of rescuing.

Badiou's ethic of truths argues instead for an abundance of immortal value. Advancing that argument, Badiou proposes three theses that stand in opposition to an economic and moral logic of scarcity. Thesis 1: "Man (sic) is to be identified by his affirmative thought, by the singular truths of which he is capable, by the Immortal which makes of him (sic) the most resilient and paradoxical of animals." Thesis 2: "It is from our positive capability for Good, and thus from our boundary-breaking treatment of possibilities and our refusal of conservatism, including the conservation of being, that we are able to identify Evil—not vice versa." And Thesis 3: "All humanity has its roots in the identification of thought [*en pensée*] of singular situations. There is no ethics in general. There are only—eventually—ethics of processes by which we treat the possibilities of a situation."[18]

Ignatieff claims that ultimately, the aim of the human rights movement is to create the rule of law.[19] But creating the rule of law poses a perplexing question for democracies: are governments, institutions, communities, and families that accord their citizens, constituencies and members security without democracy preferable to democratic governments that accord their institutions, communities, and families relatively little, if any, economic, military, civil, and political security? The answer is no longer self-evident, if it ever was. There are conditions of stability that are more deplorable than uneven chaos and partial anarchy. How such conditions are determined, who draws the lines and defines the spaces, where those lines get drawn and those places get located constitute much of the ongoing struggle between the paradoxical values and traditions of liberty and equality.

These struggles have taken a normative turn, veering away from foundational social scientific theory, moving instead in the direction of moral reasoning.[20] The (universal) human rights movement is an integral interlocutor in this normative turn. That turn draws from John Rawls's foundationalist theory of justice, Michael Walzer's communitarian critique of foundationalism, and Rawls's revisionist move toward a more particularist formulation of political liberalism. Alasdair MacIntyre's critique of universal reason in favor of a historically circumscribed ethic is intimately tied to practical life. Zygmunt Bauman's argument is that there are no foundations on which to build an ethical model (hence his starting place is the messiness of everyday life). And certainly Richard Rorty's idea of a pragmatic critical reason by means of which communities determine what is true for them, on the one hand, and on the other hand Alain Badiou's argument for an "ethic of truths" not tied in any way to a consideration of Other are pivotal points as well in the moral reasoning debates.[21]

All seem to agree in varying degrees that it is inconsistent if not unethical or evil to insist on human rights constraints for other bodies if the proponents of such constraints fail to embrace, adopt, and practice those instruments self-implicatively. Unprincipled inconsistency breeds the cynicism and resistance that currently challenges the legitimacy and coherency of the human rights movement. The critical task at this point is to review democratic arguments making human rights claims that are based on the contradictions of the liberal and egalitarian traditions. The point is to use the angry, impassioned, and at times desperate voices of the human rights debate to fashion counter-imaginaries, counter-practices, and counter-discourses capable of mediating, however temporarily, antagonistic conflicts framed by and at the same time mired in discourses of human rights.[22] These are conflicts over immanent matters in which the personal, domestic, and communal increasingly are implicated in the international, transnational, and global.

The Global and the Local

In his discussion of self-determination, Ignatieff concentrates on the tensions produced when values and interests are articulated, but as a consequence human rights and nation-state stability contradict. Nation-state stability is presumed to be the precondition for the possibility of human rights. The same tensions are at work, I argue, on the planes of personal, interpersonal, familial, and institutional experience. This section maps some of these parallel articulations of relative scale invariance. In terms of substance, planes of experience are different orders of magnitude. In terms of form, however, the analogues are more heuristically invariant than previously thought. In what follows, I read Ignatieff's analysis of national, international, transnational, and global human rights paradoxes on the planes of personal relationships, intimate partnerships, marriages, families, communities, and institutions, each of which has to reconcile human rights values and their observance on the one hand, with containing a dissident, resistant, or oppressed oppositional sentiment on the other.

Dissidence, resistance, and opposition can materialize in the embodied form of a child, a spouse, a partner, an employee, or an ethnic minority seeking self-determination, acknowledgment, and the recognition of legitimacy. Such secessionist challenges come in the forms of leaving home, running away, proposing a trial separation, a permanent separation, a divorce, a re-zoning initiative, a re-districting plan, changes to institutional charters, constitutional challenges and amendments, and anything else that may threaten the boundaries and stability of a current regime. When conflict becomes deadlocked over issues framed in terms of human rights, is it possible—and if so, how—to reframe and perhaps even resolve those conflicts? Ignatieff's explication of universal human rights, the dilemmas of positive and negative freedoms and rights, and the various critiques of the concept of rights—universal, human, or animal—shed light on the significance of thinking across planes of experience.

Secessionist challenges, whether interpersonal, familial, organizational, institutional, sub-regional, regional, national, or international often provoke terrorism, murder, violence, and the threat of violence administered by a current regime of power during crises of legitimacy. Physical abuse, emotional abuse, spiritual abuse, and sexual abuse (often densely intersecting forces and reality-effects) include the discursive and non-discursive practices of yelling, cursing, pushing, shoving, slapping, punching, kicking, biting, choking, throwing, hitting, shooting, and stabbing. Damaging property and animals are common practices for inducing terror. And incarcerating, restraining, abandoning in dangerous places, neglecting, refusing help when sick or hurt, depriving of food and sleep, physically isolating and threatening to kill are all common forms of torture. Threatening to harm self, children, or others; denying access to support; stalking, degrading, accusing, blaming, lying, breaking promises, destroying trust, and other forms of intimidation are invoked on any level of administration, as are the practices of limiting reproductive freedom, including use of birth control, inflicting pain during sexual intercourse, and raping. Such terrorism is sponsored at the international, regional, sub-regional, national, state, local, institutional, communal, familial, and relational planes of experience, and is almost always administered in the name of stability and unity, as ways of avoiding the dissolution of the arrangements and relations of the status quo on which rights-based claims are grounded.

Regarding the issues of secession, separation, divorce, autonomy, sovereignty, and independence, consider the following post-colonial reality-effects. Amnesty International reports that seventy-three percent of the emergency room visits by battered women occur after separation from a violent partner/husband.[23] Seventy-five percent of the calls made to police regarding domestic violence occur after separation. Abuse of battered women and children may sharply escalate at the time of the separation, as fathers attempt either to reclaim the family or to retaliate. Forty plus children are abducted by a parent each hour in the United States, more than half occur in the context of domestic violence. More than eighty percent of the abductions by parents occur after separation.

What are the pragmatic consequences of invoking human rights discourse in the midst of such conflict on any plane of analysis? If the objective of conflict resolution and reconciliation is to stop or at least to curtail abuse and violence, does the deployment of human rights discourse accomplish that objective? It is not a question of disputing that humans *ought to* have certain rights recognized and acknowledged; although, some would contest this moralized implication. Rather, it is a question of whether making that morally grounded argument, founded as it is on human rights values and deployed as it is by means of human rights discourse, actually produces a reduction in abuses and violations of human rights.

The dilemma lies in how to meet secessionist challenges—most often changes proposed in the name of more democratic, human rights-based relationships/regimes, complete with enhanced autonomy even if not full sovereignty, and individual agency even if not complete self-determination—without resorting to blatant repression that publicly sacrifices the façade of human rights. The threat of instability to a nation-state, community, family, marriage, or partnership is the most frequently relied upon justification for totalitarian, authoritarian, fascistic, and democratic regimes to deploy such practices. Secessionist challenges in the form of leaving, running away, ending, destroying, or any other form of dissolving a union, are used by regimes on whatever scale consisting in whatever constitution to justify authoritarian, patriarchal, abusive, violent, totalitarian, and fascistic domination and rule.

One irreconcilable problem in Western human rights policy is that promoting ethnic self-determination—or personal agency and individual human rights, for that matter—more often than not threatens the stability of forms of governance and the contents of values that supposedly found and protect those rights. The reterritorialized presuppositions of essentialized common sense are threatened by the deterritorializing effects of self-determination and personal agency, threatening to tribalize and collectivize the relatively stable, reterritorialized identity of a regime. System stability, whether or not it is productive of the rights of its constitutive members, is taken to be a necessary precondition for protecting those rights.

Ironically, the human constituencies, whose rights the system's stability supposedly protects, must of necessity violate those rights in the course of protecting them. The rights of the majority trump the rights of the minority in the name of protecting the individual. Constitutionalism on the juridical plane of the nation-state, and enforceable contracts on the legal plane of the domestic-state, imply a reterritorializing and an overcoding of the identities of unions. This produces a tightening of the articulation—i.e. a reterritorializing—of relatively loosely coupled and deterritorialized unions of peoples, states, and nations. And on the domestic plane it produces a loosening of the relatively tightly coupled unions of one (presumably heterosexual) spouse, two (presumably heterosexual) parents, one marriage (presumably legal), and so on.

Communalization, which implies both familiarity and intimacy, also implies servitude and hostage-taking, both inevitabilities in poor countries, dysfunctional marriages, violent families, divided communities, and predatory institutions in which the patriarch remains the major source, often the only source, of economic security. The threat of ethnic, personal, and spousal violence dramatically increases in such circumstances. An independent civil society, not unlike an independent individual life, is one of the frames on which are hinged the political-economics of multi-ethnic pluralism and constitutionalism, predicated as they are on mutual respect of foundational differences and a commitment to equally binding rules of engagement.[24]

Human Rights Discourse and Immanent Conflict in Copenhagen

I lived in Denmark for much of 2003–04, prior to the much heralded cartoon controversy, dividing my time between urban Copenhagen and rural Jütland. I worked with a variety of human rights groups and conflict resolution/management communes sponsoring intercultural mediation and dialogue services. We were tasked with designing a variety of communication processes and alternative interventions to address the escalating intensities of affect and libidinal conflicts between predominantly Social Democrat Danish nationals, Christian Democrat Danish nationals, Muslim Danish nationals, and Arab Muslims in search of citizenship, work permits, and asylum. Social Democrat governmental human rights agencies were funded and operated under the auspices of a conservative Christian Democrat Danish national government. Independent conflict resolution and management communes and academically housed mediation programs were also involved.

The first of two issues most directly in conflict at the time concerned young (i.e. pre-teen and early-teen aged) girls in forced marriage arrangements leaving their families of origin and arriving at Danish government-sponsored human rights agencies asking for, in effect, cultural (not political) asylum.[25] At the time, this was a relatively unprecedented phenomenon and the Danish government and its human rights agencies had next to no explicit policies in place capable of sorting this out. The second issue being hotly contested at the time was the Arab Muslim Danish national and Arab Muslim communities pressing for the construction of a mosque in Copenhagen and for several others throughout Denmark.

How to proceed? A variety of communicative processes and extra-institutional fora and venues were being designed and debated. Insofar as much of the communication between and among the various factions had been mediated largely by newspapers, television, and increasingly by the internet, there was an emerging consensus that a first step might be to create spaces where these communities would have an opportunity to speak the truth of their experiences of living in contemporary Denmark and working with its ever-changing multicultural and multilingual challenges and opportunities. And every bit as important was an opportunity for these conflicting factions to listen and perhaps even to witness one another. Language translators, cultural translators, and multicultural mediation teams played pivotal roles in these deliberations, and an even more pivotal role in the "gatherings," as they came to be called, that followed.

These gatherings resembled a hybrid of Rwandan *gacaca* outdoor community courts, and small scale, informal, indoor and outdoor truth and reconciliation commission proceedings. I worked primarily as a low-level assistant to whoever needed a hand.[26] My two most important contributions may have been first, sharing my experience of working with polygamous mothers and their children, health department officials, and several Utah state legislators. In Utah, polygamy is practiced as a sacred article of faith by Fundamentalist Latter Day Saints (FLDS) whose largest community is in Southern Utah bordering Arizona. The children were not being vaccinated for fear that the family patriarch would be identified by the health department, arrested, tried, and incarcerated, leaving the wives and children destitute. Polygamy in Utah is illegal, but tolerated for a whole host of complex historical and cultural reasons.

My second value as a resource for my Danish and Arab colleagues was that as a result of my negotiation, mediation, and dialogue work with FLDS women and children, healthcare officials and state legislators regarding basic medical care, I had begun rethinking and reimagining the conventional wisdom of much of conflict resolution and conflict management theory and practice. Frankly, much of it was too simplistic and naïve to be of much practical use. I brought most of my FLDS field note journals, and journals of notes I had taken as I was reading rather far afield from conventional liberal-humanist and neoliberal negotiation, mediation and dialogue texts. My Danish and Arab colleagues—my mentors, really—found these two resources valuable as we collectively made our various ways down unmarked paths in our collaborative efforts to articulate the various Danish factions to one another.

"Gatherings" were intended as informal, community spaces in which Danish nationals—Christian, Muslim, and atheist—and non-Danish nationals—Christian, Muslim, and atheist—of very different cultural heritages were welcomed and all were invited. These "gatherings" began very modestly, in terms of interest, trust, attendance, and participation. They began with Danish and Arab Muslim members of multicultural and multilingual mediation communes talking about the struggles they encountered and continue to encounter living as Muslims in Copenhagen with Copenhagen's Socialist Democrat human rights agencies and Denmark's conservative Christian Democrat government. Beginning with and focusing on stories, and later on longer narratives of lived experience, was one way of avoiding, at least initially, the problems I discussed earlier in this paper of relying heavily on abstracted and transcendent human rights discourse. More specifically, the focus of most of these stories and narratives was on the truth of personal lived experiences about the challenges of living day to day as a Muslim—Danish national or not—as a member of a diasporic community in a northern European, largely Christian nation-state.

Danish nationals—both Muslim and Christian—had an extended opportunity to witness the stories and narratives of Arab Muslims rather than recording and processing singular complaints and collective grievances. No commentary or discussion followed each story, many of which were partial, fragmentary, and allusions to much more complex narrative histories. Instead of engaging in policy based, legally framed, and conceptually abstracted deliberations, truths born of traumatic events began to emerge, hesitantly at first. Later, questions were allowed at the discretion of the narrator on condition that the asker did not know the answer. In other words, leading questions were discouraged, and the narrator of whom the questions might be asked was free to ignore any and all questions, or to respond in any way to questions the others asked.[27]

Formatting these gatherings as "witnessing" rather than as discussions, meetings, town halls, deliberations, hearings, or grievance proceedings avoided, at least for a time, impersonal, abstract, rights-based, positioned discourse. The multi-cultural mediation teams involved were in no way trying to suppress intensely emotional stories and narratives of "evental" experience, nor were they trying to deny human rights in any way, nor were they merely "talking about" human rights and its attendant implications. Rather, they were actually *doing* (i.e., enacting, performing) human rights discursively, immanently, in singular material circumstances, and in ways that addressed singular truths to be witnessed.

To use Badiou's thinking, human rights discourse comes to function as an ideology of ethics by assuming that the Truth of human rights is—or certainly ought to be—a universal generality to be shared with (i.e., imposed on and adhered to by) everyone, especially (in the case of Copenhagen) Arab Muslims living in Copenhagen and throughout Denmark whose ethical codes and moral practices differ dramatically in some very important and significant ways from those of many non-Muslim Danish nationals. An "event" such as the trauma and shame of having a young promised Muslim daughter leaving home and thereby violating time-honored values and traditions, threatens family honor and Muslim sociocultural integrity, standing, and identity. Such an "event" often reinforces and reinvests a superhuman (i.e., immortal) ethic of truths for Arab Muslims, and not infrequently Danish Muslims.

Universal singularities of truth, adherence to their fidelity, care with their discernment, and restraint from the terror of their imposition is of paramount importance and significance at that juncture. The all-to-common consequence is to render an ethic of truths born of an "event" as a morality of Universal Truth. An ethic of good/bad becomes a morality of Good/Evil. And doing Good to Evil cannot but produce the Evil of terror.[28]

The challenges facing the multicultural, multilingual mediating teams in Copenhagen working in these immanent conditions of enormous subtlety and complexity amounted to finding ways of witnessing intensely libidinal, emotionally driven, and ontologically true stories. Such witnessing began very slowly and hesitantly to convoke enough conditional trust that non-Danish diasporic Muslims became sufficiently willing to grant members of the mediating team openings to ask questions. These questions, in effect, were utterances from outside the narrative monologues, utterances foreign to those monologues. Such utterances, in effect, were bits and pieces of dialogue inserted into narrative monologues. A modernist analogue for this post-humanist process of intervening into narrative monologues with bits and pieces of dialogue capable of giving at least partial voice to nascent character development (i.e., subjects in discursive subject positions) would be writing a novel somehow collectively. As characters emerge in the narrative of a novel, they do so in and through dialogue. An author is narrating a monologue of stories or a nested set of stories, and the dialogue of characters as they appear and begin to develop transforms a narrative monologue into a narrative with dialogue, i.e., a novel, a discursive genre with enormous potential to move well beyond chronicles and recitations.[29]

Narratives of "evental" truths usually assume the form of a monologue. As discursive interventions are allowed into such narratives, dialogue is interjected and those narratives become more porous and malleable, i.e., more protean. It is during processes of intervening into narratives with dialogue (i.e., utterances of those witnessing a narrative) that affirming multiple "evental" truths of partisan, singular and absolutely distinct universalities become possible. Witnessing, rather than merely waiting and then rushing into a narrative with a speaking turn, is a particularly challenging discipline in multicultural, multilingual long-term conversations, negotiations, mediations, and dialogues.[30] It is by means of patient witnessing, having spent considerable time identifying suitable venues for different discursive formations to be performed, that the coming-of-the-Same is even a virtual potentiality.

The objective of all of this communicative labor is to transform the immanent moments of virtual potentiality into discursive spaces of actual possibility, to open narrative monologues of "evental" truths to discursive interventions of dialogue, and to the possibilities of alternative forms of discursive and non-discursive processes. These are some of the challenges of enacting and performing a post-humanist communication ethic of truths in the immanence of conflicting material realities of incommensurable differences; those differences, when in conflict, are often coded in terms of universal human rights violations. However, this domain of love, art, science, and politics that confronts a post-humanist communication ethics also opens onto very different and unconventional topologies of inquiry, practice, and intervention. Unconventional discursive labor that actually *does* (i.e., performs and enacts) human rights rather than merely refers to it and represents its effects, requires both *praxis* and *phronesis*—the articulation of theory to practice, and ingenious practical wisdom.

Notes

[1] I would like to thank Bryan C. Taylor for encouraging me to submit my manuscript for consideration in this Special Issue of CCCS. The ideas, arguments and perspectives are my own and are not a reflection of his thinking.

[2] Michael Ignatieff, *Human Rights as Politics and Idolatry* (Princeton, NJ: Princeton University Press, 2001). For three essays with direct bearing on this point see Alistair M. Macleod, "The Structure of Arguments for Human Rights," Rex Martin, "Human Rights: Constitutional and International," and David Duquette, "Universalism and Relativism in Human Rights," in *Universal Human Rights*, ed. David A. Reidy and Mortimer N.S. Sellers, (Lanham, MD: Rowman & Littlefield, 2005), 17–77.

[3] Ignatieff, *Human Rights*, 21.
[4] Mark Tushnet, "A Critique of Rights: An Essay on Rights," *Texas Law Review* 8, no. 2, May 1984, 1360–406.
[5] Ibid., 1364–71.
[6] Tushnet, 1371–84.
[7] Ibid., 1384–94.
[8] Ibid., 1394–402.
[9] For a more extensive discussion of other-wise, see Leonard C. Hawes, "Becoming Other-wise: Conversational Performance and the Politics of Experience," in *Opening Acts: Performance in/as Communication and Culture*, ed. Judith Hamera (Thousand Oaks, CA :Sage 2006), 23–48; see also Gilles Deleuze, *Pure Immanence: Essays on a Life*, trans. Ann Boyman (New York: Zone Books, 2001).
[10] Ignatieff, *Human Rights*.
[11] Amy Gutmann, "Introduction," in *Human Rights in Politics and Idolatry*, ed. Michael Ignatieff (Princeton, NJ: Princeton University Press, 2001), vii–xxviii.
[12] Ignatieff, *Human Rights*.
[13] Arnold Mindell, *Sitting in the Fire: Large Group Tansformation Using Conflict and Diversity* (Portland, OR: Lao Tse Press, 1995), xv.
[14] Ibid., 73.
[15] Ibid., 75.
[16] I would like to thank the reviewer for her/his close reading of my manuscript and her/his thoughtful critical concerns about my use of Badiou for my "post-humanist" critique of human rights discourse. "What happens if a theorist or an activist wants to carry out a post-humanistpolitics but doesn't share Badiou's commitment to the Platonic idea of truth ...". I would like to point out that Badiou's commitment is not to a Platonic idea of truth, but rather to mathematics in general and to open set theory in particular. See Alain Badiou, *Deleuze: The Clamor of Being*, trans. Louise Burchill (Minneapolis: University of Minnesota Press, 2000), 66–76; see also Alain Badiou, *Infinite Thought. Oliver*, trans. Feltham and Justin Clemens (New York: Continuum, 2005), 1–28.
[17] Alain Badiou, *Ethics: An Essay on the Understanding of Evil*, trans. Peter Hallward (London: Verso, 2001), 9.
[18] Ibid., 16.
[19] Ibid., 20.
[20] Reinhart Koselleck, *Critique and Crisis: Enlightenment and the Pathogenesis of Modern Society* (Cambridge, MA: MIT Press, 1988).
[21] See John Rawls, *A Theory of Justice* (Cambridge, MA: Harvard University Press, 1971); John Rawls, *Political Liberalism* (New York: Columbia University Press, 1993); Michael Walzer, *Spheres of Justice: A Defense of Pluralism and Equality* (New York: Basic Books, 1983); Alistair MacIntyre, *After Virtue* (London: Duckworth, 1981); Zygmunt Bauman, *Postmodern Ethics* (Oxford: Basil Blackwell, 1993); Richard Rorty, *Proceedings and Addresses of the American Philosophical Association* 53: 719–38; and Alain Badiou, *Ethics*.
[22] See Gustavo Esteva and Madhu Suri Prakash, *Grassrooms Post-modernism: Remaking the Soil of Cultures* (London: Zed, 1998).
[23] Amnesty International, *Rights for All: Country Report, the USA* (London: Amnesty, 1998), 13–14.
[24] Ignatieff, *Human Rights*, 33.
[25] For a thorough discussion of these cultural, political, economic and historical dynamics see Ann Sørensen and Emily Gayong Setton, "No Safe Haven: Iraqi Asylum Seekers in Denmark," *Human in Action Denmark*, (3 July 2008), at http://www.humanityinaction.org/docs/Reports/2008-DK-reports/HIA-report-AnnSorensen-and-Emily-Gayong-setton.pdf.
[26] The Gacaca court is one component of a system of community justice established in Rwanda in the wake of the 1994 Rwandan Genocide. The Gacaca courts grew out of the Garara court

system of traditional cultural communal law enforcement procedures. Gacaca courts are a form of transitional justice designed to promote healing and moving on from the crisis. For a more detailed account see Gacaca Courts in Post-Genocide Rwanda (http://socrates.berkeley.edu/~warcrime/Papers/webley-thesis.pdf). Full report on the Gacaca courts in Rwanda by Radha Webley of University College Berkeley War Crimes Study Center 2005.

[27] This particular communicative practice we borrowed from the Quaker process referred to as a Clearness Committee. A Clearness Committee is constituted when a member of a Quaker community asks particular other members to be in service to him or her. The member asking other members to serve on a Clearness Committee asks because he or she is confronting a dilemma, a difficult decision, or a problem of some kind that remains unresolved. The members asked to participate are to ask only questions for which they have no answers. The purpose of this process is to support the thinking, clarifying, and decision making of the focus person. There are other conditions, such as a particular form of confidentiality, that pertain to a Quaker Clearness Committee that we did not borrow for the "gatherings" in Copenhagen.

[28] Were there space enough and time, I could argue that such a characterization describes the historical arc of the development of The Declaration of Human Rights following the Second World War.

[29] I have in mind here many of the ways Mikhail Bakhtin theorizes some of the ways Dostoevsky wrote his novels. See particularly Chapter 5, "Discourse and Dostoevsky," in *Problems of Dostoevsky's Poetics*, trans. Caryl Emerson (Minneapolis, MN: University of Minnesota Press, 1984), 181–269.

[30] For a much more detailed discussion of these challenges see Bernard Mayer, *Staying with Conflict: A Strategic Approach to Ongoing Disputes* (San Francisco, CA: Jossey-Bass, 2009). Although Mayer is not addressing post-humanist critiques of human rights discourse, his discussions of the many paradoxes of such pragmatic work is quite valuable.

Exiled Writers, Human Rights, and Social Advocacy Movements in Australia: A Critical Fugal Analysis

Ruth Skilbeck

Whereas much work in cultural and communication studies of "the subject" and subjectivity in language has focused on deconstructive theory and critique disconnected from actual practice and people, this paper applies an innovative cultural studies approach to a journalism reflective practice research project, conducted by the author, into human rights advocacy for cases of exiled writers in immigration detention centers in Australia. In the intellectual context of "counter-hegemonic" theories that use music as an analogy for affective social relations, the paper applies what is herein termed a "fugal critical analysis," by drawing on both musical and psychological meanings of fugue (as musical counterpoint and psychological loss of awareness of self-identity following trauma) to discuss a human rights research project. The project includes conducting interviews with an exiled Ivory Coast journalist, and an Iranian poet-musician, and their advocates, including founding member of PEN's Writers in Detention committee whose publication of an exiled writers' anthology helped secure their releases on a case by case basis. The paper argues that direct engagement with cases of social injustice—here crystallized in the encounter of the interview—brings new relevance to cultural studies research practice that can effect significant changes in perception and action; in this case shifting consideration of "the subject" from the much publicized hypothetical "death of the author" of recent theory, to actual cases of exiled endangered writers, bringing cultural studies research into institutional spaces where cases can be humanely heard and supported, not merely critiqued and deconstructed.

Action Writing

> The need to detain an unlawful non-citizen should be assessed on a case-by-case basis, taking into consideration the circumstances of the individual concerned, rather than mandating detention for all individuals who fall within certain broad groups. (Migration Amendment (Immigration Detention Reform) Bill 2009. Submitted by the Australian Human Rights Commission, to the Senate, 31 July 2009)[1]

Shifting modalities, from the "reader" to "action writer," produces a dis-position to social agency and action in cultural and critical studies research. Demonstrating such a shift, this paper reflexively deploys an innovative creative practice methodology—herein termed *fugal critical analysis*—to discuss a case study of journalism reflexive practice into cases of exiled writers in immigration detention centers in Australia. The methodology is situated within the intellectual historical context and terminology of counter-hegemonic, or contrapuntal, approaches that allude analogously to the social relations and affect enacted in the form of musical counterpoint, for example Said's "contrapuntal analysis,"[2] and Bakhtin's "polyphony" and "dialogism,"[3] that can also be extended to concepts of "counter-readings" in, for instance, Foucault's critical discourse analysis.[4] Fugue not only exemplifies musicalized counterpoint and polyphony; it is a multivalent cultural figure with another, distinctive, psychological meaning—loss of awareness of self-identity, coupled with a wandering journey—that significantly informs fugal critical analyses (precedents include Julia Kristeva's concept of "abjection" and her interpretation of Bakhtin's "carnivalesque" in literary form[5]). The discussion focuses on *how* the practical application of a *fugal*, critical/cultural studies approach can be productively used in contemporary social contexts to critically analyze and at the same time actively advocate for—and intervene on behalf of—"cases" where human rights laws of freedom of opinion and expression, intersect with the rights of refugees and asylum seekers. The paper's argument is developed through a critically reflective account of research into contemporary cases of a number of exiled writers, political refugees who were held for years in immigration detention, and advocacy movements in Australia including PEN Australia, International PEN (an acronym for Poets, Essayists, Novelists), non-government organizations (NGOs), and grassroots activist movements whose sustained case by case lobbying—of government and at the Refugee Tribunal—eventually helped secure release of the writers.

The case studies are taken from a research project the author undertook into media representation of refugee writers between 2007 and 2009. The research for this project involved the reflective practice of writing interview-based media articles on writers who were exiled due to their writings that exposed official corruption, putting their lives in danger in their undemocratic homelands. On arrival in Australia during the years of the "Pacific Solution" and met with mandatory indefinite detention and temporary protection visas, they were each held for years without trial in detention centers. The interviewed writers included a former Ivory Coast political journalist and an Iranian poet-musician, both of whom are now permanent residents of Australia. This paper discusses articles published from this research in a new media outlet, *Homepage Daily*, "Make Art Not War" (a 750-word experimental mixed-media piece) and "Refugee Writers Beyond Detention" (a 2,500-word factual reportage story).[6]

The case studies discuss effective Sydney PEN interventions, including starting up the Writers in Detention Committee and publication of *Another Country: Writers in Detention* in 2004[7] edited by novelists Rosie Scott (author of *Faith Singer*) and Thomas Keneally (author of *Schindler's List*), which helped secure release of all the writers in the anthology. In 2004, PEN was awarded a Human Rights Community Award for its work in helping to raise public awareness of asylum-seeker issues in Australia. As part of the research the author made contact with founding members of the committee and interviewed Dr Rosie Scott.[8] In critically exploring and developing this theme, the paper analyses discourses of social movements of refugee advocacy and activism that grew in response to the policies of the Pacific Solution (1999–2007), mandatory indefinite detention, and temporary protection visas. The author interviewed advocates and activists on their practices of advocacy including involvement in tribunal cases. Field research included attending events with advocates and activists, visiting poetry readings, writers' festivals, and Villawood detention center. Taking this methodology one step further, the paper suggests that such dialogic research practice can effectively focus on particular cases and play an active part in resistance to hegemonic structures, through active *resistance for* the advocacy of democratic freedom of expression in a range of media, thereby playing an active role in advocacy that may intervene in particular cases and at the same time reasserting the active social and cultural role of the public intellectual.

The broader social context in which this methodology is developed and deployed is the (re)turn to both distributive and recognition justice, discussed here particularly in reference to new politics of social inclusion and calls for new conceptual frameworks and terms for articulating what have been termed the "relational aspects" of social inclusion: "culture, ethnicity, racism and other diversity signifiers as a causal factor of disadvantage."[9] The significance of using musical analogies in cultural criticism and social theory is that music constitutes an expression of social relations, whether in actual or transcendental (ideal) form;[10] as it is through relationships that people are products of society and a part of it.

The fugue (from the Latin *fuga* for flight), is the exemplary contrapuntal and thereby relational musical form as it proceeds by way of counterpoint, or interweaving voices (an instrument can be a voice), in relational response to each other. In its dialogic application, the performative fugal methodology is informed by methods including Said's contrapuntal reading[11] across cultures; Bakhtin's polyphonic dialogism;[12] Bhabha's cultural hybridity,[13] or the mixing and interweaving of cross-cultural references in the production of texts; and *écriture feminine*, the 1970s movement of women's writing and art in women's voices.[14] Fugue, which has origins in antiquity in the singing voice evolving in the form of the round, potentially enacts a form for infinitely many diverse voices, a form of democratic cultural conversation that creates a form coded and constructed reflexively by the "melody lines" that each participating voice takes up, interpretively playing variations on the theme. This suggests a useful arts-based analogy for expanding cross-cultural conversations for many voices in the mediated globalizing world.

Yet the fugue has a second "psychogenic" meaning of dissociation: as a wandering journey of temporary loss of awareness of self-identity. As dissociative disorders are increasing in an era of globalization,[15] this is used not only as a cultural metaphor but for the practical purpose of developing knowledge for advocating for the rights of exiled writers in relation to effects of cultural and psychological trauma. This aspect of the methodology is informed by feminist post-Freudian psychoanalytical theories that explore the unconscious function of writing as a form of restitution of a lost object.[16] This is a rich field for cross-disciplinary inquiry in relation to the contradictory, mediated impacts of globalization,[17] and further informed by contemporary trauma theories, including recent work on cultural trauma following September 11,[18] and recent literary trauma theory.[19] This is referred to in relation to cultural trauma and collective identity formation, informing subliminal practices of social inclusion and exclusion through processes of cultural memory and cultural amnesia that may be articulated in writing. Foucauldian discourse analysis of institutional power informs the framework and underpins the inquiry.[20] Together, these interpretations inform the cultural studies methodology deployed in the media practice theorized here.

Writing Action

Fugal critical analysis relates to a new research field of multimodality[21] that constructs meaning as an assemblage of perceptual, conceptual, and material elements; the methodology is phenomenological, i.e., based on experience. This paper develops a concept herein termed *contrapuntal writing*. In constituting a relationally based critical/cultural theory of social inclusion, the paper argues for and re-positions a focus from the contrapuntal reader to a *contrapuntal author* who is an active social agent. Several functional shifts occur in the transposition of focus from the reader to the writer. This, crucially, includes a shift from a *de dicto* (about) to a *de re* (of) relation of modality of intentionality (relation to objects of thought) of the researcher to the objects of research. A *de dicto* relation is one of about-ness, *about* an object of thought. It is a relation of second-hand "knowledge" or information, and received ideas. A *de re* relation is a phenomenological relation of the "subject" (researcher/active writer) to objects based on a phenomenological experience gained directly through (multi-modal) sense perception. This adapts Brentano's theory of intentionality.[22]

Part of a "modal" shift from reading *about* to one of active writing *of,* basing on the researcher's experience, is a shift away from a theory based on metaphor to one that is empirically based on experience of phenomena through sensory perception. This modal shift produces, for example, a shift from the term "exiled writers" used as a metaphor (such as the "death of the author" or "dissolution of the unified subject") to a phenomenological-based analysis of actual cases of exiled writers—based on face-to-face interviews with writers in exile. This shift produces not only an awareness but also, in varying degrees, an engagement with the social and cultural contexts of the writers' exiles. But it is also an awareness of their situation as human beings who may still be suffering the after effects of the trauma of exile and detention. This produces a very different kind of research process and knowledge than the one based only on "reading." Phenomenological experience impacts upon the researcher and causes reflexive affects, which can be quite profound and can motivate a deeper level of engagement. Such direct involvement turns the "objects" of research into living "subjects" with subjectivity and human identities and can lead to taking up and advocating for individual cases, as occurred with the exiled writers discussed here.

Journey into Exile

In terms of the psychological aspects of the fugue, analogously the form relates to origins of language formation in the body, in the unconscious that Julia Kristeva referred to as the "pre-semiotic chora."[23] Reference to the non-representational, fugal, musicalized language of literary art is relevant to the origins of the case studies of the exiled writers. The journey described in the next part of this paper was an active development and application of research into the writer's fugue: *musicalization, trauma, and subjectivity in the literature of modernity*,[24] which discovered a link between uses of fugue form in musicalized writing and authors' experience of trauma—including the experience of exile.

Some of Western modernity's most innovative and profound writers and artists were propelled by traumatic experiences of loss to create innovative fugal language works—including de Quincey (*Dream-Fugue*), Proust (*À la recherche du temps perdu*), Joyce ("Sirens" in *Ulysses*), Celan (*Todesfuge*), and Plath (*Little Fugue*). This related to a phenomenon observed in research into ways that individuals and communities may recover from trauma through the practice of innovation.[25] Writers may symbolically and literally re-make themselves, and create or join new communities in the process of writing. The fugal modality of writing involves a paradoxical loss of awareness of self-identity: a temporary experience of dissociation and yet at the same time, a process that may constitute re-membering or re-construction of a fragmented self.[26]

Fugal Approach

Fugue serves not only as a multi-modal analogy, but also suggests a number of critical style terms transposed from music, as outlined below and applied to a fugal analysis of the cases:

- *Fugal Modality:* In the *fugal modality of writing* two theories of modality are brought together. The first derives from the philosophical concept of modality and modal logic, and is related to the concept of *de re* thought as articulated in linguistic propositions. The second is derived from modal music and is related

to re-writing language as creative art. How it works can be conceptualized imaginatively. It is the modality of creative psycho-linguistic re-invention in any medium of language and (potentially) infinite variation on a theme.
- *Fugal Recursion:* A concept of reflexivity, which "puts on hold" one voice, whilst another picks up and plays the theme.
- *Polyphony:* Many voices.
- *Counterpoint:* Interweaving of "voices" (not necessarily verbal, a visual image or effect can be a "voice").
- *Variation:* Fugue proceeds through variations on the theme including elaboration, embellishment, distortion, inversion, mirroring, repetition, diminishment.
- *Double Counterpoint:* A relational aspect of force is implied, as in carnivalesque, parodic satirical discourse or dialogue, in which the dominant voice switches place with the subordinate, and vice versa.
- *Dialogism:* Bakhtin's term for the interplay and intertextuality of voices in cultural productions.
- *Recurring Motifs:* An image, a shape, a sound: a signifier of un/conscious subliminal or subtextual psychological or cultural motive.
- *Memory Involuntary:* Memory and loss of awareness of self identity that constitutes an a-semantic link in the creative processes of composition, particularly in the "inspirational" mode of compulsion to make art. Paradoxically this process of invention from memory also involves forgetting in a form of fugal recursion. This may be applied to the phenomena of cultural memory and cultural amnesia.

Cases of Exiled Writers and International Human Rights Law

Article 1 (A2) of the UN Declaration of Human Rights defines a refugee as being "a person who ... owing to a well-founded fear of being persecuted for reasons of race, religion, nationality, membership of a particular social group or political opinion, is outside the country of his nationality and is unable or, owing to such fear, is unwilling to avail himself of the protection of that country." It is this definition that has been incorporated into Australia's 1958 Migration Act.[27] Australia is a signatory to the 1951 Refugee Convention relating to the Status of Refugees and its 1967 Protocol. Yet the Australian Human Rights Commission has consistently contested the most stringent immigration policies from Australia aimed at deterring asylum seekers from approaching the country, policies that were implemented between 1999 and 2007:

> The Commission has consistently called for an end to the mandatory detention system because it places Australia in breach of its obligations under the International Covenant on Civil and Political Rights (ICCPR) (1966) and the Conventions on the Rights of the Child (CRC) (1989) to ensure that no one is arbitrarily detained (8.48 Migration Amendment (Immigration Detention Reform) Bill 2009. AHRC Submission to Senate).[28]

The policies of the so-called "Pacific Solution" created migration "zones of excision"—excising the northern coastal borders and waters from Australia's "migration zone" to deter arrivals of asylum seekers by boat on the north coast. Those in the excision zone could not access Australia's migration determination system, and have been transferred to Papua New Guinea or the Pacific island of Nauru.[29] This followed what is known as "the Tampa incident:" when a Norwegian ship that had rescued asylum seekers from a sinking boat brought them to Australia, as the nearest country, and was refused permission to land. At the same time, policies were implemented of mandatory indefinite detention and Temporary Protection Visas (TPVs).

Asylum seekers arriving without a visa (including accompanied and unaccompanied children) were classified as "non legal non citizens," and held in mandatory indefinite detention. This included those who arrived by plane or by ship at a city port (like the exiled writers in the case studies).

If they were granted refugee status, "non legal non citizens" were granted only three-year Temporary Protection Visas, in contrast with "legal non citizens" arriving in Australia with visas, who were granted Permanent Protection Visas.[30]

"Temporary Protection" meant a state of chronic indeterminacy. In detention, political exiles and asylum seekers were homeless and stateless in a zone of psychological and physical limbo. This state of limbo produces trauma and has serious effects for the mental health of exiles and detainees. Immigration Detention Centers were in isolated areas, including the desert, surrounded by razor wire, e.g., the notorious Woomera Immigration Reception and Processing Centre in the South Australian desert (closed in 2003). Suicide attempts, self harm, and desperate acts such as lip sewing were everyday occurrences. Suicides occurred, as did fires, protests, hunger strikes, and occasional break outs. As a sign of their official dehumanization the detainees were numbered, and called by their numbers for head counts every few hours throughout each day and night.[31]

> As far as history goes in Australia, it was one of the worst periods ... It was the complete abnegation of their human rights. They weren't even allowed a trial. (Dr Rosie Scott, in interview with the author)[32]
>
> in Woomera ... 400 people shared two toilets. (Steven Biddulph, psychologist)[33]
>
> A child attempts to hang himself with a bed sheet on playground equipment.
>
> A child on hunger strike.
>
> A child found in razor wire again.[34]
>
> If you want to close your eyes, to not see what happen in the world, you become blind. (Mohsen in an interview with the author)[35]

The impacts of this environment on mental and physical health are extensively documented in *A Last Resort, National Inquiry into Children in Immigration Detention* by the Australian Human Rights Commission (formerly Human Rights and Equal Opportunity Commission). Impacts are also documented in advocates' reports in books, articles, and on websites through NGOs, and many groups and individuals that make up the social movement of refugee advocacy in Australia.

If you close your eyes you cannot see. You cannot close your heart. You cannot close your ears. If you want to close your mouth, ear, heart. If you are heartless, you have no emotion. You are going to be a robot. And not be human. (Mohsen)

How important was poetry to you in detention?"

It was like breathing. (Mohsen)

(Writer 1)—The way they treated us was disgusting ... The way they practice their interview techniques like no respect at all. And not that: we know that you come from a difficult situation, we can help you now, but we need to find out what really happened. There was nothing like that. It was like: why the hell did you come here in the first place, you know? Yeah, I think that was one of the main things that people felt that they were so, you know, unwelcome. That no matter what they did ... Yeah that was really key to the whole story.

And so the opposite kind of reaction from other people on the outside helped to counter-act that?

(Writer 1)—Yes. That attitude of hey, we believe you, you know we want to hear your story. Tell us what happened and how you are feeling. What can we do. Yeah, not much we can do about it, but what do you think we can do, and just people saying, I'll send you a phone card so you can contact your family. Things like that. And that's when PEN, they did start helping. Wanted to find out what's was happening. And from then on the story was more public.[36]

It was in the zone of indeterminacy and uncertainty in 2001 when PEN founded the exiled writers, who had begun to send out messages from detention, including Cheikh Kone's newspaper called *Freedom*. Kone, a political journalist from the Ivory Coast, produced this newspaper with a group of detainees on a computer in Port Hedland Immigration Reception and Processing Centre (detention centre) and faxed it to Amnesty International.

Deconstructing Dehumanization and Deviancy

Foucault drew attention to the kind of foreclosure of technical instrumental rationality that operates in "rational" systems such as prisons. On his account we can be seen to be living in an "episteme"[37] where the immigration detention center was an institution where the power/knowledge intersection was enacted in an authoritarian practice in which exiles were routinely "dehumanized" as a matter of implementation of policy. Their individual cases were not considered, and they were left in limbo for years before their cases were brought to the Refugee Tribunal (where over eighty percent of detainees were found to be refugees, and given TPVs[38]).

Such institutional responses of the episteme of postindustrial late modernity constructed a response that has an affective dimension that may generate fear and paranoia. Sharon Pickering analyzed media discourses on asylum seekers and refugees, concluding that they were routinely constructed not only as a "problem" population but as a "deviant" population in relation to the nation state, race, and disease. She argued that this is systematic and endemic to the construction of "normalcy in prevailing social orders and the reproduction of hegemony." She concluded that "frameworks of deviancy help us to unpack the way asylum seekers can be put on trial by the media without the power to narrate their own stories."[39]

The power to tell stories about oneself is intrinsically related to a sense of self-identity. It is in many respects what makes us human. Yet, negative stereotyping and misinformation about "illegal immigrants" relayed through the media caused a counter response in the form of strong refugee advocacy movements that spread across Australia.

The cases of the exiled writers in the case studies were taken up by PEN, a group that lobbied tirelessly for their release. "Poets, Essayists, Novelists" is an international humanitarian organization of writers that started in London in the early twentieth century to lobby for the rights of imprisoned writers around the world. In 2001, Sydney PEN formed the first Writers in Detention committee when members found out that there were exiled writers held in immigration detention centers in Australia. PEN's influential writer members, including novelist Thomas Keneally and some journalists including David Marr, put out strong messages in the media through articles, broadcasts, and books that drew attention to their plight.

In the international return to recognition justice, the Australian Human Rights Commission has, in its latest submission, called for case by case assessment of those detained as an "unlawful non-citizen." The Commission states: "While the initial detention of unauthorized arrivals might be legitimate on these grounds, this must be for a minimal period, and be proportional [to legal and safety concerns].[40]

The renewed focus on the individual is very significant. The humanity and success of the PEN campaign for the writers in detention was that the writers were humanized as individual cases. They were exiled for that very reason of expressing their views as individual authors: practicing the right to freedom of expression and free speech with the aim of exposing corruption for the benefit of their communities.

Refugee Writers: Beyond Detention

Mohsen

Mohsen is an Iranian poet and musician who fled Tehran after he wrote pieces that tried to expose corruption. In Australia he was detained in Port Hedland and Villawood detention centers for four years. When in Villawood, Mohsen met several advocates who took up his case, including Rosie Scott and Tom Keneally. He made two CDs, with a number of prominent people in Australian arts and politics, who recited his poetry recorded with his own music. All the proceeds from the CD sales went to Chilout, the organization that lobbied to end the detention of children.

In two interviews at his home in inner Sydney, Mohsen talked about the trauma that he had experienced and how this had affected him.[41] Even though he had been released three years before under medical advice, he still could not work full time. He was finishing a surveying course at a Sydney college of Technical and Further Education (TAFE). He had fled Iran after exposing corruption: "For my political activism I became endangered. I came to Australia by plane to Perth." He had thought that he was going to Perth in Scotland. When he arrived he was put into Port Hedland Detention Centre and moved to Baxter Detention Centre. He said: "There were five people to a [small] room with two beds ... if the door opened [it] banged you on the head." Following a protest, detainees were sent to prison for a few months. In comparison, he said: "when I went to prison it was wonderful. Everything was good. The doctor—we could see. In 18 months I hadn't seen any doctor, any specialists. I was in a very, very bad condition." After three years he was transferred to Villawood Detention Centre in Western Sydney. In total he spent four years in immigration detention.

The article, written after speaking with Mohsen, entitled "Make Art Not War" is a piece of experimental arts writing. It is written in the "voice" of Rosa Viereck, art critic and abstract expressionist artwork, in a column entitled Pink Oblong (Rosa Viereck is the title of a painting by Vasily Kandinsky). Yet the story was clearly ascribed to the author in a copyright attribution at the end of the story. The multimodal story also included a photo of Mohsen reciting poetry at the poetry reading. The story began:

> Australia, or Invasion Day, makes me think of geometric shapes. Black squares. White cubes. Me. In a gallery. A pink oblong. My own shape. Rosa Viereck: pleased to meet you.

The abstract, fragmented voice continues:

> I'm secure in my identity. But sometimes just the sound of the word Australia, let alone its abstraction, can make me question who I am. "Where do we come from? What are we? Where are we going?" was modernist artist Paul Gauguin's heartfelt cry in "French" Tahiti. His painting's plea becomes an epithet to colonial identity confusion.

Interweaving in a multimodal fugue:

> ... I am looking at the symbolic shape of what is known as an icon of Australian identity art. Sidney Nolan's outlaw: Ned Kelly. Riding through a desert. Gun in hand. In reverse. A symbol of quixotic alienation: human form reduced to a black abstraction in the red heart. White settler alienation in a black helmet. What are we? What does it mean to be Australian? It's a familiar refrain. Can we find ourselves through Art? I am here to tell you, yes, and lose ourselves as well. Look at me! And look at Nolan ...

The dissociated voice of Rosa Viereck, abstraction personified, drew a connection between unsettled Australian artists, indigenous women activists and exiles in detention in the desert:

> Looks like he found out a thing or two as he lost himself in a hallucinogenic landscape of his own perception. About the shifting shapes of "settler" identity. The outlaw. The colonial law enforcers.

The voice stops and starts, breaks and continues:

> *But things have changed since Nolan painted his Kelly series in the late* 1940s. *The modern era has shifted to postmodernism. Multiplicity abounds. Polyphony rocks. In the new era of protest, outlaws are replaced by activists. Fighting for social justice for outsiders "othered" by the ex-colonial law makers. Refugees in detention.*

Indigenous communities. Stranded in 21st century deserts. Deprived of health and education services settler society calls basic. When activists faced charges—later dropped—of helping refugees escape the country to a third country of refuge, writer and refugee supporter Tom Keneally wrote to those facing court: "The better angels of Australia are singing with you."

The story was intertextual, quoting from an artwork and from:

> Another Country, writers in detention, edited by Tom Keneally and Rosie Scott.
> I open at random, and read:
> In the midst of parched desert
> No one can come with us
> We cannot journey hand in hand
> There is no green place to rest the eye
> And the scorching wind of destiny lashes at our backs
> A call to DIMIA is a like the smell of rain in the desert
> Hope, like black clouds, building in our thirsty hearts
> Turns quickly to grief ...

The deconstructed narrative ended with an exhortation:

> In the great southern land we are all at heart dislocated, invaded and invaders. Together, we can reshape the future. Through mutual acceptance of many colours and shapes. Reconciliation. Make Art not War.[42]

Why take this approach? Affected by Mohsen's story and by the anguish of his poetry, this drove an attempt to inhabit more deeply the imaginative and affective space that Mohsen described in his poetry, his music, and his conversation. Visualizing this space—of trauma, isolation, and displacement—in the paintings of Sydney Nolan in a retrospective of his works at the Art Gallery of New South Wales at that time. Hearing it in the words of indigenous speakers on Human Rights Day; weaving together these multimodal threads in an abstract piece on cultural trauma and identity on Australia or Invasion Day. The multimodal article was published with photographs of Mohsen, Aunty Shirley an indigenous rights activist, and an image of Nolan's Ned Kelly painting.

Cheikh Kone

Cheikh Kone was a young journalist in the Ivory Coast, working for *Le Patriot*, when his life became endangered after he wrote articles critical of government elections. He was forced to flee. Concealed under a blanket in a four-wheel drive car driven by a friend of his father, over the border to Ghana, and then to Benin, where he was given berth on a ship. And after a long and dangerous journey via South Africa, he stowed away on another ship (and, as he says, believing it was bound for Europe), then he arrived in Australia. A story he tells in *Another Country*.

Whilst in detention, Cheikh was adopted as International PEN's first "writer at risk" and was the first asylum seeker in Australia to have his case "internationalized by PEN."[43] Taking up his case when he was under consideration of deportation to the Ivory Coast, PEN centers around the world contacted the government. The PEN

Submission to the Human Rights and Equal Opportunity Commission for the Community Services Award (2004) states: "Eventually, through the work of many groups and individuals, including the PEN Australia centers and International PEN and their network of associated writers and human rights advocacy groups, Cheikh was released this year after spending three years in detention."[44] He was released in 2004; and after gaining his Law degree, he is working as a field officer in a union, "looking after public servants," and is married with a child.

In detention, he continued to actively write. At Port Hedland Detention Centre he and some other inmates started up a newspaper. He said:

> We had a committee management that said we could have a newsletter. We were allowed to have a computer at least a couple of hours every day so we started a little newspaper called *Freedom*. We did only three issues, once a month ... People who got their visas were leaving and I smuggled a copy out so people could read it on the outside. I faxed a couple of copies to Amnesty International overseas ... Some Australian people [from outside] got involved knowing what we are doing—and I asked for and I got my own computer, and so then I started to write, a story ...[45]

The journalism story was written in a factual reportage style designed to give maximum opportunity for Cheikh to tell his story in his own voice. Cheikh Kone said in an interview that "the catalyst" for his still being sane, after almost four years in detention centers, was communication with people from the outside:

> I really made sure that I was in contact with people as much as possible. I spent *hours* on the phone and also talking with people in that environment with people that showed me that I wasn't worthless. Because being in detention give you this sense of being worthless. You're not at home. You're not where you want to go. You're not in prison. See, it's just, it's the middle of nowhere, that feeling. So just being in touch with people, talking to people in the community was really, really important, just that verbal communication with people and their letters. And then people, like saying, yeah we know how you feel, even though we're not there, and we believe your story. In any case [if] not true, we just want to make sure that it's given...we want to hear your story ...[46]

The PEN submission to the 2004 Human Rights Community Award stated: "While Cheikh's case ignobly signalled the first time Australia was included in International PEN's infamous Writers In Prison publication, because of the manner and scope of refugee detention in Australia and the advocacy of the PEN Australia centres, the Australian Government has come under more sustained international pressure than any other country over this issue."[47]

Changing Policies

Changes have been made to refugee and asylum policy in Australia since 2004. The Rudd Labor government began to disband the Pacific Solution in 2007. In 2008, Temporary Protections Visas were replaced with Permanent Protection Visas, and detention is recommended only as a last resort and for the minimum time for processing asylum seekers (rather than as a punitive "deterrent"). The newly renamed

Australian Human Rights Commission—which was called the Human Rights and Equal Opportunities Commission until August 9, 2009—has a public website where Submissions and Reports are accessible, as is a detailed account of the recent history of changing refugee human rights policies. Further amendments are under submission.[48]

In September 8, 2009, The Migration Amendment (Abolishing Detention Debt) Bill was passed through the Australian Senate. Australia was the only country in the world where asylum seekers were charged for the cost of their mandatory detention; a policy introduced by the Keating Labor government in 1992, which "had proven to be highly ineffective and heartless."[49] On their release, refugees were given huge bills. For some families it was over $200,000. "Those unable to pay their debts were left with an outstanding debt to the Australian Government which saw them included on a Movement Alert List. This prevented them from traveling or ... from applying to be reunited with family members overseas."[50] In the case of Cheikh Kone this had unforeseen negative effects, when, in 2004, after his release he was invited to speak at International PEN's Congress in Barcelona. He was refused a visa by the Department of Immigration at the last minute, as he had a detention debt of $89,000 dollars.[51] Although at the time nothing could be done, this is further evidence of the importance of a case by case approach, for the carriage of social justice for the individual.

Fugal Analysis

Throughout this discussion, fugal terms have been referred to in accounts of the dialogic, polyphonic communication between the exiled writers and their advocates, in relation to the communication of the advocacy movements, and the phenomenological practice of the research project. Fugal concepts are deployed in a cultural analysis of the communication—between the advocates and the exiled writers and in the wider context of Australian society in a process of ongoing social, cultural, and institutional change. To draw out a few of the terms, specifically the fugal aspects in the case studies include:

- *Fugal modality of writing:* The "voice" of the text is significantly dissociated from the author. The story is carnivalesque, exhibiting modes of parody and satire driven by a deeper sense of social injustice, and clearly articulated affect of trauma. Interwoven through the written text are striking modes or "voices" of visual communication: images of artwork and photographic portraits. Fugal recursion occurs in the "putting on hold" of one voice (written text) whilst another voice (visual communication) interprets the theme in a different way. This creates a counterpoint of voices. The double counterpoint occurs in the parodic subversive intertextual modality of inter-discourse. The story's dialogism operates on several levels of cultural, social, political, historical and art historical discourse.

    In the second story, the fugue may be interpreted to include elements of non-verbal communication in the dialogic performative encounter of the interview.

The fugue of the dialogic exchange comprises the look in Cheikh's eyes, the tone of his voice, certain hesitations and accelerations, when he says: "It is a long time since I have spoken of such things" or "I never usually talk of this." An intensity of wordless gestures. A poignancy and strength. And grace of spirit, expressed through the language of the body, in the time of the interview.

- *Dialogism:* The broader fugue is that of the dialogic communication between the advocates and their exiles, the polyphonic communication that occurred in the multiple forms and modes of exchange and interaction including letters, faxes, phone calls, visits, non verbal, and empathetic communication between advocates and exiles.
- *Counterpoint:* Occurs in the interweaving of the voices in this fugue, the exiled writers, the advocates and activists (and adversaries) it occurred through dialogue, performance, writing, telling stories.
- *Double counterpoint:* Occurs in the communication between dominant voices and marginalized voices, of the exiles and their advocates, that throughout the process of the "exiled writer's fugue" changed places as the writers were freed and gained permanent residency (and the policies of mandatory detention and TPVs have now been rescinded).
- *Cultural memory and amnesia:* Many have commented on the anomaly of Australian refugee policy that, in effect, repeats in a distorted form the origins of the colony as an off-shore prison for convicts and undesirables that was settled by incoming boat people. But, to adapt a Foucauldian influenced trauma theory, this may be understood as a systematic return of the repressed. The "immigration processing centre" in the desert literally and symbolically articulating a (non)"processing" of trauma. Cultural trauma theory suggests that such trauma may be caused by guilt. A Freudian analysis in "Remembering, Repeating and Working Through"[52] would suggest that automatic forms of repetition may only be resolved if the traumatic "memory" is worked through or processed consciously in the culture. Eerie echoes of the origins of the colony, return—such as a traumatic repressed memory, a recurring nightmare- in the shape of the detention centre in the desert ...

Fugal Reflection

Taking an active writing research approach gives the opportunity for critical cultural studies to actively investigate individual cases of exiled writers, exploring issues of writing and rights. In effect this occurred in the journalism reflexive practice discussed here, which was informed by recently updated UK and Australian journalists codes of ethics and guidelines, including the National Union of Journalists "Reporting Issues of Refugees and Asylum Seekers."[53]

A main conclusion to emerge from this research is the vital importance of restoring a sense of the human value of the subject and the author, in theory as in practice. For this research shows what happens when the subject is under threat of erasure through "dissolution"—when even a name is replaced by a number. Without a sense of the worth of individual personal identity, the subject does dissolve. But that occurs as the result of trauma, the taking away of human rights of freedom of expression and free speech. Self-based narratives and story telling are essential components to building a strong sense of self identity that is necessary to write actively and effectively albeit that may be in disguise or through an alter ego, in contrapuntal, parodic, or carnivalesque forms.

Replacing a "model" of the passive reader/viewer with an active writer produces a very different effect and ethic of experiential engagement, including experimentation, innovation, and discovery. This may lead to writing: a book, an article, a film, a documentary, creating an event in the public sphere, transforming and processing trauma in creative cultural production.

Notes

[1] Australian Human Rights Commission, http://www.hreoc.gov.au/
[2] See Edward W. Said, *Culture and Imperialism* (New York: Vintage Books, 1993); and *Musical Elaborations* (London: Chatto and Windus, 1991).
[3] Bakhtin coined the terms dialogism and literary polyphony as concepts of character (and subject/self) developed in dialogue with others in his analysis of Dostoevsky in *Problems of Dostoevsky's Art*, later translated into English as *Problems of Dostoevsky's Poetics*; elaborated in *The Dialogic Imagination: Four Essays*, ed. Michael Holquist, trans. Caryl Emerson and Michael Holquist (Austin, TX and London: University of Texas Press, 1981).
[4] Producing a counter reading of social conditions offering possibilities for critique and change; see *Les mots et les choses* (Paris: Editions Gallimard, 1966) trans. A. M. Sheridan Smith as *The Order of Things* (London and New York: Routledge, 2002); and *L'Archéologie du savoir* first published by Editions Gallimard in 1966, trans. A. M. Sheridan Smith as *The Archeology of Knowledge* (London: Tavistock Publications, 1972).
[5] See Kristeva's literary-cultural analysis in *Pouvoirs de l'horreur* (Paris: Édition du Seuil, 1980) trans. Leon S. Roudiez as *Powers of Horror: An Essay on Abjection* (New York: Columbia University Press, 1982); on the carnivalesque "Word, Dialogue and Novel" in *The Kristeva Reader*, ed. Toril Moi (Oxford: Basil Blackwell, 1986).
[6] Ruth Skilbeck, "Refugee Writers: Beyond Detention," http://Homepagedaily.com 3/5/2009; "Make Art Not War," http://Homepagedaily.com 3/2/2008.
[7] Rosie Scott and Tom Keneally, ed., *Another Country: Writers in Detention* (Sydney: Halstead Press, 2004).
[8] Including Professor Denise Leith author of *Bearing Witness: The Lives of War Correspondents and Photojournalists* (Milsons Point: Random House, 2004). In 2006, Rosie Scott was awarded the Inaugural Sydney PEN Award for her work including foundational work in forming the Writers in Detention Committee. One commendation was that: "she has shown how a writer can be a powerful activist" Sydney PEN Award (http://www.pen.org.au).
[9] In Hurriyet Barbacan's Plenary Speech "300 Days: Social Inclusion and the Rudd Government," *Rights, Reconciliation, Respect, Responsibility: Planning for a Socially Inclusive Future for Australia Conference*, University of Technology, Sydney, October 2, 2008.
[10] Ruth Skilbeck, "Art Journalism and the Impacts of "Globalisation": New Fugal Modalities of Story-telling in Austral-Asian Writing," *Pacific Journalism Review* 14 (2008): 141–61.
[11] See Said, *Culture and Imperialism*.
[12] Mikhail Bakhtin, "Forms of Time and the Chronontope in the Novel," in *The Dialogic Imagination: Four Essays*, ed. Michael Holquist, trans. Carl Emerson and Michael Holquist (Austin, TX and London: University of Texas Press, 1981/2004).

[13] See Homi Bhabha, *The Location of Culture* (Abingdon: Routledge, 1994).
[14] Leading practitioners include Hélène Cixous, Luce Irigarary, and Julia Kristeva.
[15] Hence psychogenic fugue is the focus of medical research, e.g., Michael D. Kopelman, "Focal Retrograde Amnesia and the Attribution of Causality: An Exceptionally Critical Review," *Cognitive Neuropsychology*, 17 (2000): 586–621; and Hans J. Markowitsch, "Functional Neuroimaging Correlates of Functional Amnesia," *Memory* 7, (1999): 561–83.
[16] Julia Kristeva, *Powers of Horror: An Essay on Abjection*. trans. Leon S. Roudiez (New York: Columbia University Press, 1974/82). Luce Irigaray, *An Ethics of Sexual Difference*. trans. C. Burke and G. Gill (Ithaca, NY: 1983. Melanie Klein, *Love, Guilt and Reparation and Other Works 1921–1945 by Melanie Klein* (London: The Hogarth Press, 1930/75).
[17] For instance in Judith Squires, *The New Politics of Gender Equality* (London: Palgrave/Macmillan, 2007).
[18] See, for examples, chapters by Jeffrey C. Alexander and Piotr Sztompka, in *Cultural Trauma and Collective Identity* (Berkley, CA: University of California Press, 2004).
[19] See, for example, Cathy Caruth's *Unclaimed Experience: Trauma, Narrative and History* (Baltimore, MY: John Hopkins University Press, 1996); and Caruth's *Trauma: Explorations in Memory* (Baltimore, MY: John Hopkins University Press, 1995).
[20] Michel Foucault, *Discipline and Punish: The Birth of the Prison* (London: Allen Lane, 1973).
[21] Theo Van Leeuwen and G.R. Kress, *Multimodal Discourse: The Modes and Media of Contemporary Communication* (London: Edward Arnold, 2002).
[22] Brentano Franz, *Psychology from an Empirical Standpoint (1 & 2)*, Linda L. McAlister, ed. trans. Antos C. Rancurello et al. (New York: Humanities Press, 1973).
[23] Julia Kristeva, *Powers of Horror: An Essay on Abjection*, trans. Leon S. Roudiez (New York: Columbia University Press, 1974/82).
[24] Ruth Skilbeck, *The Writers Fugue: Musicalization, Trauma and Subjectivity in the Literature of Modernity*. PhD thesis. Library, University of Technology, Sydney, 2006.
[25] Piotr Sztompka, "The Trauma of Social Change: A Case of Postcommunist Societies," in *Cultural Trauma and Collective Identity*, ed. Jeffrey C. Alexander et al. (Berkley, CA: University of California Press, 2004).
[26] Skilbeck, 2006.
[27] Australian Commission for Human Rights, http://www.hreoc.gov.au/legal/submissions/2009
[28] ACHR website at http://www.hreoc.gov.au/legal/submissions/2009
[29] ACHR website at http://www.hreoc.gov.au/legal/submissions/2009
[30] Frank Brennan, *Tampering with Asylum* (St. Lucia: University of Queensland Press, 2003).
[31] Human Rights and Equal Opportunity Commission, *A Last Resort? National Inquiry into Children in Immigration Detention*, April 2004. Australian Commission for Human Rights website, www.hreoc.gov.au.
[32] Interview with Rosie Scott, October 2007.
[33] Steven Biddulph, "LOVE is Stronger than Fear. The SIEV X Memorial," in *Acting from the Heart: Australian Advocates for Asylum Seekers Tell Their Stories*, ed. Sarah Mares and Louise Newman (Sydney: Finch Publishing, 2007), 182.
[34] Human Rights and Equal Opportunity Commission, *A Last Resort? National Inquiry into Children in Immigration Detention*, April (2004): 442–3, Australian Commission for Human Rights website, www.hreoc.gov.au.
[35] Interview with Mohsen Soltany Zand, October 2007.
[36] Cheikh Kone in an interview with the author April 2008, University of Technology, Sydney.
[37] Discussed, for example, in *Les mots et les choses* (Paris: Gallimard, 1966) (*The Order of Things*, New York: Vintage, 1973); and *Surveiller et punir* (Paris: Gallimard, 1975) (*Discipline and Punish*, trans by Alan Sheridan (New York: Pantheon, 1977).
[38] Australian Commission for Human Rights, http://www.hreoc.gov.au/legal/submissions/2009
[39] Sharon Pickering, "Common Sense and Original Deviancy: News Discourses and Asylum Seekers in Australia," *Journal of Refugee Studies* 14 (2001): 169–89, 169.

[40] Immigration (Detention Reform) Bill 220. Submitted by the Australian Human Rights Commission to the Senate, July 31, 2009. Australian Human Rights Commission http://www.hreoc.gov.au

[41] An advocate who had visited him in Villawood and remained good friends with him, introduced the author to Mohsen, at a spoken word poetry club at a basement bar in Sydney's King's Cross. Mohsen was performing spoken word poetry and playing improvised music accompanied by two men on traditional Persian instruments including sitars. Mohsen had agreed to requests for photographs and for an interview.

[42] Skilbeck, "Make Art Not War."

[43] Sydney PEN website.

[44] Sydney PEN website.

[45] Skilbeck, "Refugee Writers Beyond Detention," http://www.Homepagedaily.com. 3/2/2009.

[46] Interview with the author, April 12, 2008, University of Technology, Sydney.

[47] Sydney PEN website.

[48] Australian Commission for Human Rights, http://www.hreoc.gov.au

[49] Media release, Refugee Council, September 8, 2009.

[50] Ibid.

[51] Sydney PEN website.

[52] Sigmund Freud, Errinern, Wiederholen und Durcharbeiten (Weitere Ratschläge zur Technik der Psychoanalyse, II). *Internationale Zeitschrift für ärtztliche Psychoanalyse* 2 (1914): 485–91. In English translation: "Remembering, repeating and working-through" in *Beyond the Pleasure Principle and Other Writings,* trans. John Reddick (London: Penguin Books, 2003), 31–43.

[53] National Union of Journalists (2004/08) *Reporting Asylum and Refugee Issues,* http://www.mediawise.org.uk

The Abuses of Literacy: Amazon Kindle and the Right to Read

Ted Striphas

This paper focuses on the Amazon Kindle e-reader's two-way communications capabilities on the one hand and on its parent company's recent forays into data services on the other. I argue that however convenient a means Kindle may be for acquiring e-books and other types of digital content, the device nevertheless disposes reading to serve a host of inconvenient—indeed, illiberal—ends. Consequently, the technology underscores the growing importance of a new and fundamental right to counterbalance the illiberal tendencies that it embodies—a "right to read," which would complement the existing right to free expression.

On Friday, October 24, 2008, media mogul Oprah Winfrey went public with the details of her new love affair. It had begun innocently enough, over the summer, and her appearance that fall day on *The Oprah Winfrey Show* would leave no doubts about just how smitten she had become. There was no reason to believe Winfrey would be leaving her long-term partner Stedman Graham anytime soon, however, for the new object of her affection was just that—an object, or rather, a gadget. "Anyone who knows me knows that I'm really not a gadget person at all, but I have fallen in love with this little baby," Winfrey reveled.[1] She was referring to Kindle, Amazon.com's popular handheld electronic reading device.

Kindle had already generated substantial buzz by the time the device first caught Winfrey's eye. Within a week of its November 19, 2007 debut, *Newsweek* had featured the e-reader in a cover story entitled "The Future of Reading," and US Public Broadcasting's Charlie Rose had chatted-up the device for a full hour with Amazon founder and CEO, Jeff Bezos.[2] The disclosure of Winfrey's love affair with Kindle, a little less than a year later, was equally, if not more, significant. After all, this was not just any media personality giving Kindle her endorsement—this was Oprah Winfrey, whose book club had established her as one of the most visible arbiters of literary taste in the United States.[3]

For others, though, the love affair with Kindle has been anything but candy and roses. Consider the case of "Ian," who wrote in to the online forum *MobileRead* in April 2009 to lodge a complaint against Amazon.com.[4] As "a loyal customer," Ian claims to have purchased "thousands of dollars" worth of items from the retailer throughout the years, including a second generation Kindle.[5] But from Amazon's point of view Ian was less a loyal customer than he was a difficult one—too difficult, in fact. On April 6, Amazon customer service emailed him to say that it had closed his account due to the suspiciously high volume of refunds he had requested.[6] Ian had become too costly a customer, that is to say, and so Amazon decided to cut its losses and fire him.

This type of behavior is not unheard of in the realm of retail.[7] The side-effects of Ian's account deactivation did raise some eyebrows, however. One result was that he could no longer purchase e-books from Amazon. Ordinarily this would not have been a problem, except for the fact that Amazon is the exclusive seller of Kindle content. Another result was that Ian lost the part of his Kindle library that he had archived on Amazon.com's proprietary servers.[8] In the language of the gadget-savvy his Kindle had been "bricked," or transformed into little more than an expensive empty shell. After some negotiating (and presumably some bad publicity) Amazon.com reinstated Ian's account, albeit on a probationary basis.[9] His romance with Kindle may have finally turned a corner, but by then it was pretty clear that it would never end up a fairy tale.

It may be difficult to judge how much stock to place in Ian's story, given its origins on the internet. Corroborating it, however, is somewhat beside the point. Kindle is an example of an increasingly prevalent type of information technology—what Jonathan Zittrain calls "tethered appliances." He explains: "They are *appliances* in that they are easy to use, while not easy to tinker with. They are *tethered* because it is easy for their vendors to change them from afar, long after the devices have left warehouses and showrooms."[10] In other words, tethered appliances oblige you to enter into enduring relationships with corporate custodians, who make it their responsibility to manage the inner-workings of these devices. The bottom line is that even if Amazon never really bricked Ian's Kindle, the nature of the technology is such that the company could do precisely that—or worse.

With the endorsement of a high-profile opinion leader such as Oprah Winfrey, Kindle may well be on its way to achieving what no other handheld e-reader has managed to achieve thus far: mainstream acceptance. Indeed, a policy paper by the Democratic Leadership Council, a Washington, DC-based think-tank, urges school districts throughout the United States to switch over to an electronic textbook system architected around Kindle or a "Kindle-like device." Moreover, there is a movement afoot in universities—underwritten by Amazon—to switch over course textbooks to Kindle.[11] The release of Apple's hotly anticipated iPad in April 2010 has helped to temper some of the exuberance about Kindle, to be sure. The latter's release in the form of iPad and iPhone applications demonstrates Amazon's willingness to hedge its bets on Kindle, even by piggybacking on a competitor's hardware. So given the prospect that Kindle adoption might soon reach a tipping point, now seems like an appropriate moment in which to explore whether it would be desirable to construct the future of reading on this or some other similar platform.

If we accept Raymond Williams' claim that "[t]he moment of any new technology is a moment of choice,"[12] then the question becomes: what happens if we choose to tether reading, via Kindle, to Amazon.com? This question, it should be pointed out, has implications that exceed the act of reading itself. As Alberto Manguel notes in his *A History of Reading*: "The methods by which we learn to read not only embody the conventions of our particular society regarding literacy ... they also determine and limit the ways in which our ability to read is put to use."[13] The same thing might also be said about the *devices* people use to read, which up until recently consisted of (to impose an anachronism) untethered print-on-paper objects predominantly.[14] The latter have existed for centuries, and the habits of thought, conduct, and expression they have helped to foster have been well documented.[15] But since comparatively little is known about how Kindle may "determine and limit" the uses of literacy, it becomes difficult to make an informed decision about whether to strike up a relationship with the device, or not.

This paper attempts to remedy that. My argument is that however convenient a means Kindle may be for acquiring e-books and other types of digital content, it nevertheless disposes the act of reading to serve a host of inconvenient—indeed, illiberal—ends. My broader and related claim is that Kindle personifies a challenge to a core set of liberal democratic principles, which also happen to share an enduring association with reading in the United States. Ultimately, then, there is more to Kindle than just a smoldering obsession with a high-tech gadget. There is the need for a new and fundamental right to counterbalance the illiberal tendencies that it embodies—what some have called a "right to read," which would complement the existing right to free expression.

The Paradox of the e-book

Before getting to all that, however, it is first necessary to say something about how the public conversation regarding Kindle has unfolded thus far. It is a sprawling one, to be sure, stretching across radio, television, print media, the internet, and more. Yet for all its apparent breadth it still manages to exhibit a striking lack of depth—not in the sense that the commentary has been unintelligent, but rather in the sense that it has tended to fixate on a fairly narrow matter of representation.[16] One result has been a sidelining of the broader issue of rights.

This framing owes much to the rhetorical agility of Jeff Bezos, who is often well out in front of the news reporting on Kindle. The device's overarching purpose, as he explained in the aforementioned *Newsweek* cover story, would be to bring books—what he called "the last bastion of analog"—into the digital realm.[17] Sensing perhaps that he had overreached, Bezos later clarified on *Charlie Rose* that his company's new e-reader was not intended to "outbook the book." "Instead of trying to duplicate every last feature," the Amazon CEO stated, "we have to look for things that we can do with this technology that we could never do with a paper book."[18] Here, Bezos put his finger on what you might call the "paradox of the e-book."[19] By this I refer to the implicit belief that e-reading devices such as Kindle are at once less *and* more capable of replicating the form, function, and atmospherics—call it the experience—people often associate with printed books.

On the one hand, Kindle presents itself as demonstrably book-like—by which I mean, *printed* book-like. The box for the first generation device, which is decorated with black typography cascading whimsically across a white background, resembles in both size and shape a dictionary, encyclopedia, or other substantial reference matter. Kindle carrying cases could easily pass for fine, leather-bound journals, or perhaps daybooks, not unlike those you might find in an upscale book or stationery store.[20] Together, the box and folio comprise what Gerard Genette calls the "paratextual"—or perhaps here it would be more accurate to say "paratechnological"—elements whose purpose is to frame the perception and use of a given text or, in the case of Kindle, a given textual platform.[21] Beyond whatever utilitarian function these accouterments might serve, they are clearly intended to yoke Kindle to the visual aesthetics of contemporary print culture. Furthermore, Amazon engineered the first generation Kindle to approximate the size, shape, and weight of a paperback volume, and in doing so it endowed the otherwise sterile unit with a semblance of bookish physicality (figure 1).[22] Finally, Kindle has been widely touted for mimicking the "immersive" experience said to characterize printed book reading, thanks to its use of high-tech electronic ink developed at MIT's famed media lab. "The key feature of a book is that

Figure 1. Kindle (first generation) and its paratexts.

it disappears," Bezos has claimed, and it is precisely this level of transparency that Kindle is supposed to achieve.[23]

On the other hand, Bezos has repeatedly stressed the many ways in which Kindle will "improve upon the book."[24] The e-reader's ostensible upgrades over its predecessor include: onboard third generation (3G) mobile phone technology; 3G integration with Amazon.com, allowing readers to purchase and download electronic content on the fly; memory, capable of storing up to 3,500 e-titles depending on the model; reference features, consisting of a built-in dictionary and wireless access to *Wikipedia*; readerly amenities, including font resizing and, on newer models, a text-to-speech function; and wireless backup on the Amazon.com server cloud. Bezos' enthusiasm for talking up these and other features makes his reticence about the number of Kindles that Amazon.com has sold all the more curious. One source, reportedly with insider knowledge, claims that the company sold close to a quarter-million units between the middle of November 2007 and the end of July 2008. And while it may be imprudent these days to lend credence to Wall Street speculation, for whatever it is worth, Citigroup estimates that total Kindle sales reached three million units as of December 2009.[25]

So what are we to make of this paradox—the fact that Kindle always seems to be chasing after the printed book while at the same time exceeding it? It is telling that when Bezos mentioned the "key feature of a book," he neglected to specify the type of book to which he was referring. Indeed, he did not have to. Despite the inroads handheld electronic reading devices have made into contemporary book culture, print and paper are still very much the norm—so much so that they need not be acknowledged. According to Gary Hall this unspokenness signals the degree to which supposedly cutting-edge e-readers such as Kindle remain "tied to the ink-on-paper template," or caught within a "papercentric" worldview.[26] This also holds true from the other end, where the express goal is to "improve upon the book." Once again print and paper play the role of referents, functioning as the invisible yardsticks against which Kindle will be judged to have failed or succeeded. The upshot is that Kindle and surely other e-readers such as the Barnes & Noble Nook and the Apple iPad invite constant—even incessant—comparisons with printed books, regardless of which side of the paradox one finds oneself on.

The narrowness of the public conversation about Kindle is understandable on some level, given the custom of making sense of the new by drawing analogies to the already established. Doing so has a long and distinguished pedigree within the history of communication. At least since Plato, almost every medium has been talked about in terms of whether it diminishes or enhances the capacities of its predecessors, from the human voice to the human hand on down to the printing press, typewriter, computer, and beyond.[27] To the extent that that conversation has failed to achieve any type of consensus after two-and-a-half millennia, it may be time to recognize it for what it has become: a spirited, if ultimately reductive, analytical fallback. Walter Ong sums up the matter wryly: "[t]hinking of oral tradition or a heritage of oral performance, genres, and styles as 'oral literature' is rather like thinking of horses as automobiles without wheels."[28] Ong's point is to address a given technological artifact in its particularity—first—and then to explore the *complex* set of relations it shares with other technologies, institutions, and social actors. What if the "problem" of Kindle were restaged, therefore, to open up questions beyond the device's ability—or not—to "outbook the book?"

Into the Amazon

More important than Kindle's connection to the printed book is its connection to Amazon.com. Hence I want to return to the idea that Kindle is a "tethered appliance" and to consider the implications of that designation.

Kindle is probably the first standalone e-reader to provide for real-time communications between bookseller and consumer, thanks to its onboard 3G mobile phone technology. One result is that readers can download the complete contents of any Kindle-formatted title directly to their units in under a minute, provided that they are within range of a cell tower. It is little wonder, then, that Bezos describes Kindle as a "service" and as "an extension of the Amazon store," rather than more generically as a handheld mobile device or even more specifically as an e-reader.[29] Kindle promises not only to usher reading into the twenty-first century but also to inaugurate an era of convenient, ubiquitous bookselling.

Much has been made of these downstream capabilities, but what about the data that Kindle transmits upstream, back to Amazon.com? The company is hardly shy about the fact that Kindle gives as well as it receives. It treats the device's upstream capabilities as a selling-point, in fact, promoting them to users as a helpful way of managing content and of safeguarding the many hours they have invested in reading it. Kindle's automated "back-up" feature relays any electronic text annotations, highlights, and dog-ears that a reader may make to Amazon, in addition to other information including where in a given text she or he may have left off reading. These data are then stored in the company's vast system of computer servers, or cloud, where they can be retrieved for restoration purposes in the event that one's Kindle is lost, stolen, or erased. A related feature, called Whispersync, allows owners of multiple Kindles to migrate content and data from one unit to another using the 3G network. All such transactions must proceed through Amazon's proprietary server cloud, since the company engineered Kindle to be incapable of communicating directly with others of its kind.

The language that Amazon uses in its promotional materials to describe the flow of data upstream from Kindle suggests little more than user-friendliness, as if "back-up" and "Whispersync" existed only for the sake of helping bibliophiles to get the most out of their digital libraries. Yet the Kindle License Agreement and Terms of Use indicate that the information does more than sit there idly in the cloud, waiting for the appropriate user to log on. In the subsection "Information Received," the document states: "The Device Software will provide Amazon with data about your Device and its interaction with the Service (such as available memory, up-time, log files, and signal strength) and information related to the content on your Device and your use of it (such as automatic bookmarking of the last page read and content deletions from the Device)." Once they arrive in the cloud these and other bits of data—including any text annotations and highlights you may have made—become "subject to the Amazon.com Privacy Notice."[30] The latter, ironically, opens up quite detailed information about your personal reading habits to a host of uses beyond the express purposes of backing up and syncing.[31]

I will return to this point shortly, but first it is necessary to say a few words about the changes Amazon has made recently to its corporate identity. At the risk of overgeneralizing, it is probably fair to say that most people consider Amazon.com to be an online retailer. That is a safe enough assumption, but it is only partially accurate. The company has actively—and until the last three or four years, quietly—been making itself over into a web services provider, or even more ambitiously into a platform upon which to construct on- and offline businesses.[32]

The shift started around 2002, when Amazon began looking for ways to improve its hardware utilization. At issue was the overcapacity of the servers and other back-end computing infrastructure that supported its website, which the company had designed, or scaled, in anticipation of meeting sudden but infrequent increases in demand. As Nicholas Carr observes: "Amazon had to construct its system to be large enough to accommodate the burst of shopping during the week after Thanksgiving—even though that week comes around only once a year. Most of the system's capacity went unused most of the time."[33] Consequently, Bezos and company decided to rent out its excess computing power to just about anyone willing to pay.

Amazon.com subsequently spun off a new division of the company, Amazon Web Services LLC, or AWS. Launched officially in 2006, AWS belongs to a broader movement in the technology industry known as "utility computing." Whereas the philosophy of personal computing stresses widespread computer ownership just in case, the philosophy of utility computing perceives that as a waste of money and other important resources. Instead, the latter stresses only the barest minimum of individual computer ownership, and mostly then of web-facing devices that have been significantly downscaled in terms of both memory and horsepower. In the event that someone requires additional storage space, processing capacity, or the like, a large, centralized provider will be happy to deliver it just in time via the web, often for a fee.[34] For its part AWS offers a suite of products including: Elastic Compute Cloud or EC2, a platform for running applications on top of Amazon's proprietary computing infrastructure; Simple Storage Service or S3, a massive, secure parking lot for client data; SimpleDB, an on-demand database hosting and architecture service; CloudFront, a content storage and distribution system; and more.[35] Little wonder that Bezos has described Amazon.com not as a retailer but as "a technology company at its core."[36]

The point is that Amazon is not just the retailer that many of us believe we know. It is also becoming what *Business Week* has called "a kind of 21st century digital utility" akin to sites such as Google and Facebook.[37] Indeed it is significant that leading web developers have been building enterprises in whole or part on top of Amazon's vast computing infrastructure. Profile and background pictures for Twitter, for example, are hosted on S3. A bevy of the objects comprising Linden Labs' online virtual world

Second Life reside there as well, and they are delivered to residents via CloudFront. As of 2010, around 82 billion data objects resided on Amazon's servers, which fielded as many as six million client requests every minute.[38] Kindle's data collection efforts hardly occur in isolation, in other words. They belong to a broader corporate strategy in which Amazon's "behind-the-scenes data center services" have been taking on newfound importance.[39] The company's goal with these and other initiatives is to monetize any and all of its excess capacity and to transform idle assets—data included—into persistent, value-producing ones.

Of course, Amazon has been collecting, analyzing, and making use of customer information since its inception back in 1994. But in conjunction with its recent emphasis on web services, it soon becomes apparent that Kindle is deepening and widening the company's data-mining efforts:

- first, by allowing Amazon to drill down beyond the retail layer, a proven source for what Oscar Gandy calls "actionable customer intelligence," into the bedrock of everyday life;[40]
- second, and more specifically, by transforming people's idiosyncratic and heretofore mostly private reading itineraries into data-generating activities;
- and, finally, then, by implicating those acts in a larger system of productive relations.

The upshot is that Kindle raises all sorts of questions about propriety, and I mean that in both the older sense of the term—property—and its more modern usage—decorum. In the emerging world of tethered appliances, to whom does reading belong? To whom should it belong? What happens to reading once it becomes the object of another's persistent scrutiny?

The Propriety of Reading

The first of these issues—property—is a vexing one. On the surface it is likely to seem as though Amazon is taking something that belongs to Kindle owners—namely, the time and effort they have put into reading—and claiming partial ownership of it. Consequently, Kindle reading is apt to seem like an example of the "free labor" pervading digital network culture today.[41] Although less public compared to, say, a blog comment, a *Wikipedia* contribution, or an online product review, the digital data trail that is generated while reading on Kindle is nonetheless a type of user-generated content. It is given freely—albeit not voluntarily—by the client to Amazon, and the data in turn add value to the host site in the form of intelligence-driven features (e.g., product recommendations) and the more intangible "corporate goodwill."[42] Thus with Kindle purposive reading is doubled, resulting in an activity that is paradoxically unestranged from the reader on the one hand and yet estranged from her or him on the other.[43]

In plainer terms, Kindle objectifies reading by transforming a process into a recordable, transmissible thing. And it is precisely this existential work that invites comparisons of readers to laborers and of the fruits of their reading to personal property. But how appropriate is it to draw such comparisons, legally and analytically? For their part, US courts have been unpersuaded with arguments asserting property rights over personal information, even going as far in *Dwyer* v. *American Express Co.* (1995) as to declare the data generated by any one individual to be essentially valueless, economically speaking. Value is produced not in the act of creating or disclosing the data *per se*, but rather in the process of aggregating it with the data of others.[44] What the courts have seized upon, in other words, is the basic difference between *data*—a raw material—and *information*—a product. Kindle reading may yield the former, but it is up to Amazon and its database systems to generate the latter.

Of course, it would be foolish to deny the significant physical and cognitive demands that reading places on human beings.[45] Yet with respect to Kindle, the purpose and character of those demands will vary depending on which side of the tether you find yourself on. What looks like deliberate reading to a Kindle user is apt to look rather different from the vantage point of Amazon.com. The closest analog might well be found on the company's Mechanical Turk website, which debuted in 2005 and has since grown into an offshoot of AWS.

The name "Mechanical Turk" pays homage to a faux automaton whose chess-playing prowess captivated European audiences in the late eighteenth century. Secretly, the robot's skill derived not from any type of artificial intelligence but from a human chess master hiding inside the machine, who manipulated levers, pulleys, and magnets to create the illusion of self-directed game play. So too it is with Amazon Mechanical Turk, which the company refers to as "artificial artificial intelligence."[46] The service is essentially a marketplace for twenty-first century piecework, the core of which is things called "human intelligence tasks." These are, in Amazon's words, "questions that need an answer," or data processing tasks that the present generation of computers is ill-equipped to handle (e.g., writing product reviews, performing rudimentary research, identifying and tagging images, and more).[47] Collectively, Mechanical Turk workers comprise a flexible, on-demand labor force whose job is to respond to these questions. Compensation generally ranges from a few pennies to a few dollars per job, paid for by the party who has issued the specific information request, through the intermediary of Amazon.

I want to be cautious about stretching the analogy too far. Kindle reading does not fall within the bailiwick of Mechanical Turk work, and as I have already noted it is not rewarded monetarily. Mechanical Turk still has much to tell us, however, about how Amazon.com conceives of the labor of Kindle reading—as a human intelligence task. Each time a Kindle user boots the device and syncs it up with the Amazon server cloud, she or he is effectively responding to a series of Turk-like questions: what has this person been reading? How has this person been reading? For what length of time has this person been reading? Furthermore, once Amazon gets a hold of the data, the company is then able to aggregate it with the data of other Kindle users, thereby creating composite profiles of how Kindle users in general, as well as particular subgroups of them, read. Out of all this emerges a new—abstract—type of reading whose value resides almost exclusively in its economic instrumentality. Furthermore, as *de facto* extensions of the Amazon computing system, Kindle users come to comprise a massively distributed "artificial artificial intelligence" whose purpose is to map an ever-evolving "ambient informatics" of reading.[48] Thus they would appear to behave less like the "free laborers" with whom certain neo-Marxists have become preoccupied of late and more like assets or fixed capital—you might even say human resources, albeit in the grossest sense of the term. That is, Kindle readers are technologically obliged to *work* but without any pretense of *labor* as a socioeconomic ritual.

As to the matter of decorum: many of us were taught at a young age that it is impolite to read over someone else's shoulder. Doing so amounts to an intrusion into the reader's personal and cognitive space, or, stronger still, a violation of her or his privacy. The everydayness of this simple life's lesson belies a complicated history of readers and reading whose intellectual origins can be traced back to classical liberalism. In 1859, John Stuart Mill referred to "the inward domain of consciousness" as the locus of "absolute freedom of opinion and sentiment on all subjects,"[49] a conception of the self that has helped to frame subsequent understandings of how and why people read. Consider the twentieth century novelist Vladimir Nabokov, for instance, who claimed that "readers were born free and ought to remain free."[50] Essayist Sven Birkerts offers a similar opinion, suggesting that "[r]eading is the intimate, perhaps secret, part of a larger project, one that finally has little to do with the more societally oriented conceptions of the individual."[51] At the heart of the liberal formulation of reading we thus find sovereignty and solitude as optimal conditions. Reading conjures images of inwardness, of a self withdrawn from the material world into the recesses of the imagination—in short, of a private interiority whose boundaries are, or deserve to be, inviolate.

This conception has been criticized for the disproportionate emphasis it places on individuals; for reinforcing the belief that reading is a strictly cognitive endeavor; and for the bright-line distinction between public and private upon which it is premised.[52] I grant all of these objections, at least on a purely theoretical level. For in practice, the fact is that most readers begin to feel uncomfortable the instant they become aware of the presence of another's gaze. Like amateur contortionists we twist our bodies to escape it, like aspiring origamists we fold our reading materials to thwart the intruder's prying eyes. "[T]he text itself, protected from outsiders by its covers, [becomes] the reader's own possession, the reader's intimate knowledge," observes Alberto Manguel,[53] whose use of the word "covers" should be taken to include not only the trappings of a particular volume but also the many awkward movements we may engage in to shield it from others. This of course begs the question of what happens to reading and the broader sense of privacy with which it is associated once our books and periodicals become exposed to the world.

Herein lies the other fundamental dilemma that Kindle poses. As a tethered appliance it subjects readers and their reading habits to ongoing surveillance. This statement merits qualification, however, for the surveillance that is taking place does not perforce entail active human scrutiny—at least in the first instance. It is perhaps best described as "algorithmic" in that most if not all of the eavesdropping and data mining take place automatically, carried out by Amazon's powerful computer systems.[54] There is no conscious "doer behind the deed," in other words, beyond of course the programmers whose interest should extend strictly to the collection and not the substance of Kindle data. And yet there remain important reasons to be concerned about this type of data gathering, despite the apparent lack of active scrutiny on Amazon's part.

The crux of the matter comes down to information repurposing. In his extraordinary book *The Digital Person*, Daniel J. Solove asserts that there are few effective measures in place to control the afterlife of digital data—what he calls the "perspiration of the Information Age"—once they have been gathered.[55] Corporate privacy policies offer varying levels of protection, in most cases ensuring against egregious abuses of personal information. But on balance, he argues, these policies tend to be full of loopholes and exceptions that render them dangerously leaky.

For its part, Amazon states that it may transfer customers' personal information to affiliate businesses in the event of mergers or acquisitions, but pledges that it "remains subject to the promises made in any pre-existing Privacy Notice."[56] So far so good. The problem, however, stems from the practicalities of delivering on such promises when personal information flows from one large organizational, technological, or policy setting into the next. Privacy "drift" is one well-documented outcome, in which compliance with an institution's express privacy goals falls off or becomes ineffective the further that personal information migrates from the party who had collected it initially.[57] This can happen for any number of reasons, including the failure to align differing institutional attitudes toward privacy; the aggregation of personal information with data from other organizations that in turn heightens or exposes the information's sensitivity; and the declaration of bankruptcy, where an organization is legally compelled to liquidate valuable assets—databases included—in order to settle accounts with its creditors.[58] Given Amazon's sprawling corporate holdings,[59] alignment and aggregation clearly are important concerns. Moreover, Amazon's early profitability issues and the extent to which the company continues to be leveraged financially mean that its long-term solvency is hardly a foregone conclusion.

Perhaps even more troubling is Kindle's potential to render users vulnerable to unprecedented levels of government surveillance of their everyday reading activities. Despite the courageous efforts of librarians and bookstore owners, loan records and sales receipts are well-established mainstays of criminal investigations. Here the assumption on the part of government officials is that evidence of *what* a suspect has been reading may ultimately help them to establish a pattern of behavior leading up to a crime. What is important to note is the legal standard that applies in such cases. Typically, investigators need only go as far as to acquire a subpoena to access a suspect's library or bookstore records. In contrast to search warrants, subpoenas are issued by prosecutors who, like the police, maintain a strong interest in catching criminals and are thus predisposed to honor the latter's requests. Judicial oversight often "amounts to little more than a rubber stamp."[60] But accessing a suspect's own library of printed books for evidence of *how* she or he has been reading is a different matter. In the US a Fourth Amendment "probable cause" standard generally applies, which means that investigators must go through the more stringent motions of obtaining a search warrant from a magistrate.[61] The increased standard is commensurate with the privacy expectation that obtains in one's reading activities.

Kindle, however, runs afoul of the liberal belief in the sanctity of reading and hence the impulse to safeguard the sovereignty of readers. According to the Amazon Privacy Notice: "We release account and other personal information when we believe release is appropriate to comply with the law."[62] This statement is not altogether unusual. What is unusual, though, is the nature of the personal information that Amazon maintains in the case of Kindle users, namely, the bookmarks, highlighted passages, annotations, and so forth that I have previously mentioned. Amazon possesses detailed records of not only *what* but indeed *how* Kindle users read—information that ordinarily would be subject to Fourth Amendment protections against unreasonable searches and seizures. But because these data are transmitted electronically to the company and then archived in its computer cloud, US federal law considers them to be not pieces of private information but instead "stored communications." This is a special genre of information that the law considers to be beyond the scope of the Fourth Amendment, because it is shared with and maintained by a third party.[63] The upshot is that the everyday reading itineraries of Kindle owners suspected of crimes are subject not to the probable cause/warrant standard but instead to the more relaxed requirements of obtaining a subpoena. It is doubly cruel that Kindle's architecture is such that users have no choice but to allow their civil liberties to be undermined in this way.

Conclusion: A Right to Read

In June 2009, seventeen-year-old Justin D. Gawronski was already anticipating the start of his senior year at Eisenhower High School in Shelby Township, Michigan. His Advanced Placement English teacher, anxious to hit the ground running come September, had issued a summer reading assignment, and so Gawronski did what any honor student worthy of the name would do: he promptly bought the book and got right down to work. Rather than purchasing a print edition of the required reading, however, Gawronski decided to download it wirelessly onto his Kindle 2, which he had bought expressly for school. Over the next few weeks he carefully read his way through about the first third of the e-book, bookmarking pages, highlighting passages, and typing in notes in preparation for the start of the fall term. But when Gawronski booted up his Kindle on Friday, July 17, 2009, he was dumbstruck to see the volume that he had been reading disappear from the device. It had been deleted remotely by Amazon. All that remained of the e-book were his bookmarks, highlights, and notes, now rendered useless absent the text to which they once referred.

About that text: Amazon had pulled not just any book from the young man's Kindle, but George Orwell's paranoid novel of life under totalitarianism, *1984*.

Needless to say, more than a few Big Brother analogies followed in the wake of the incident's revelation in the news media.[64]

Unfortunately, it was not an isolated case. It was later revealed that the text had been uploaded onto Amazon.com's servers by a company called MobileReference, who did not possess US publishing rights to the electronic edition of *1984*. Amazon, fearing a copyright infringement suit, responded by wiping the file not only from Gawronski's Kindle but from the Kindles of everyone who had downloaded it, subsequently issuing refunds for the purchase price. The resulting public relations fiasco led CEO Bezos to issue a frank public apology, calling the company's actions "stupid, thoughtless, and painfully out of line with our principles."[65] Six weeks later Amazon decided to restore the vanished volumes; if an affected client were no longer interested in the book, then she or he could opt for a thirty dollar check or gift certificate instead. It is worth mentioning that this goodwill emerged only after Gawronski and another Kindle owner, Antoine Bruguier, had filed a class-action lawsuit in United States federal court seeking damages from the company for trespass, breach of contract, and more. Amazon eventually settled with the parties for $150,000.[66]

On one level, I am inclined to agree with Bezos' characterization of Amazon's actions as "painfully out of line with [its] principles." As an internet retailer, Amazon surely understands the importance—indeed, the value—of building and maintaining trust with clients dispersed throughout the globe. On another level, however, the statement also signals the degree to which it has yet to come to terms with its existence as a technology company. Amazon.com still perceives itself as though it were primarily a purveyor of things rather than a maker of them. As such, it does not appear to have fully thought through the implications of releasing a device such as Kindle onto the world, let alone of all the back-end database and computing infrastructure to which the appliance is tethered. What should be apparent from the foregoing discussion is that while Amazon does take steps to protect its clients as consumers, its own policies, practices, and electronic reading products, taken together, can compromise some of their basic rights as laborers and citizens.

This is an ironic situation given the name, Kindle. It harkens back to the myth of Prometheus—the Titan who, in Aeschylus's play *Prometheus Bound*, brought fire to humanity, along with mathematics, medicine, metallurgy, and other knowledge that helped free us from the absolute power of humanity's rulers, the Greek Gods.[67] Thus, with Kindle, Amazon has channeled one of the most enduring fables of human liberty, only to stand it on its head. What happens when a people either chooses or is compelled to read on a device that is so connected electronically that it manages to disconnect that people from some of the key tenets of liberal democratic culture?

In raising this question, I do not mean to imply that Kindle's success is a *fait accompli*. With new electronic reading devices now being released from Apple, Barnes & Noble, Sony, and other developers, stiff competition clearly lies ahead on the horizon. Like Kindle, however, the competition is also moving in the direction of wireless connectivity, which would suggest that in the coming years tethering is likely to become more the norm than the exception among e-readers.[68] I would venture to speculate that as these devices become even more prevalent, we are likely to witness further instances in which those who control literacy's electronic infrastructure will overstep the bounds of liberal propriety, either purposefully or accidentally.[69] How then are we to safeguard the many freedoms—social, psychological, intellectual, political—with which reading has long and productively been associated?

One proposal comes in the form of a comment on a website where I solicited feedback on a much earlier version of this paper. Evoking the Situationist approach of "*détournement*," or "the 'highjacking' and reorganization of cultural and textual materials for purposes of ideological criticism,"[70] an anonymous interlocutor wrote:

> Kindle owners could conceivably organize a sort of demographic noise-bomb by "reading" books interminably, taking nonsensical or deceptive notes on their Kindle "books," and otherwise scrambling the data gathered by the device. [Hence they would be using] the device in a way that could perhaps detour the discursive production of reading as object, returning reading to the realm of practice and invention (even if mischievous invention).[71]

I will admit to being intrigued by a course of action such as this, given its resonance with the "tactical" forms of resistance that are familiar to practitioners of cultural studies.[72] I am, however, ultimately unpersuaded by the prospect of "détourning" electronic reading devices and thus the companies to which they are yoked. Doing so may introduce a modicum of noise into the latter's databases. (This of course presumes an extraordinary level of organization on the part of those who use electronic reading devices.) Yet, as a mode of political intervention, the practice of *détournement* does little to preserve—let alone enhance—the forms of propriety that Kindle and devices like it have done their part to squander.

Put differently, techno-cultural solutions are unlikely to mitigate the actual or potential abuses of literacy that emerge in a world where reading is tethered to corporate databases. Those solutions may game the system, but in the end they still operate well within its confines. The late liberal political theorist Isaiah Berlin addresses the matter pointedly: "[I]f democracies can, without ceasing to be democratic, suppress freedom," he asks, "what would make a society truly free?" He responds with two conditions: "First, that no power, but only rights, can be regarded as absolute;" and second, that those rights should become "so long and widely accepted that their observance has entered into the very conception of what it means to be a normal human being."[73] The shift of emphasis that Berlin proposes here—namely, to rights—may seem somewhat unusual to media and cultural studies scholars who have long championed the cause of cultural politics. Yet, it anticipates recent theoretical work that has attempted to resituate culture in relationship to economics, and especially the law.[74] What this body of scholarship shows—and what the case of Kindle also underscores, I believe—is the way in which economic imperatives and legal considerations have become more deeply implicated than ever in routine cultural practices, such as book reading.

The connection between reading and liberal political culture is a contingent—not a necessary—one. It is an always fragile union forged out of historical circumstance,[75] and it promises to weaken and maybe even dissolve unless steps are taken to strengthen it in perpetuity. Legal scholar Julie Cohen, for her part, has argued that what is needed to secure the sanctity of reading in the wake of technologies like Kindle is nothing less than a "right to read."[76] Such a right, she contends, is grounded in the right to free expression, as codified in the First Amendment to the United States Constitution. "Freedom of speech is an empty guarantee unless one has something—anything—to say ... [T]he content of one's speech is shaped by *one's response to all* prior speech, both oral and written, to which one has been exposed."[77] Reading, in other words, is an integral part of the circuitry of free expression; the one simply cannot exist without the other. To the extent that a society maintains an interest in safeguarding free expression, it follows that it must also maintain an interest in safeguarding its enabling conditions.

Cohen goes even further, however, suggesting that the right to read should include the ability to do so anonymously. Reading has always been an expressive activity in its own right, resulting in dog-eared pages, marginalia, and other types of communicative fallout.[78] But tethered appliances clearly raise the stakes of this expressivity. When a reader's private scrawl is no longer secreted away in the odd corner of a random volume but is instead archived in third party databases, where it is identifiable and accessible, one must wonder what will happen to the expressive circuitry of a people. Cohen rightly fears that it could be short-circuited, pointing to "the likely chilling effect" that ubiquitously "exposed" reading would have on a people's willingness to select, access, and engage reading materials, controversial or otherwise.[79] "[A] right of freedom of thought and intellectual inquiry ... necessarily includes [I would even say, demands] the freedom to read unobserved."[80] This is currently impossible with Kindle, regrettably, since Amazon offers users no choice but to opt-in for the device's "backup" feature.

The urgency of establishing a right to read exceeds even these concerns. Over the last two decades new technological protection measures (e.g., digital rights management software) and tighter intellectual property laws have combined to roll back more than a few of the ways in which people routinely make use of book and other types of content.[81] In the process what Lawrence Lessig calls a "read–write" culture has endured a forcible makeover, to the point that it is beginning to resemble a "read-only" one—this of course assuming that people will continue to read more or less as they have, once they discover that their anonymity can no longer be assured.[82] It is important to bear in mind that these broader changes have been wrought largely by corporate media giants such as Disney and lobbying groups such as the Motion Picture Association of America, who have been aided and abetted by legislatures all too eager to appease them.[83] What a right to read might help to put in place, then, beyond the freedom to enjoy an e-book without someone peering over your shoulder, would be "a strong pro-reader default."[84] Think of it as a legal touchstone whose purpose would be to represent readers *in absentia*, in contexts where their interests might otherwise be forgotten or inadequately accounted for.

On its own, Kindle is not an abusive lover. It is nothing more and nothing less than a gadget, as Oprah Winfrey called it, albeit something of an enthralling one. The network of legal, technical, and economic forces to which it presently belongs, however, does manage to expose Kindle users to all sorts of abuses of literacy. And those abuses are likely to continue—escalate, even—absent the protections of a right to read.

Notes

[1] "Oprah's Favorite New Gadget," *The Oprah Winfrey Show* (October 24, 2008), http://www.oprah.com/slideshow/oprahshow/20081024_tows_kindle/2 (accessed July 4, 2009).

[2] Steven Levy, "The Future of Reading," *Newsweek* (November 26, 2007): 58–64. "Jeff Bezos Interview," *The Charlie Rose Show* (November 19, 2007), Lexis-Nexis [transcript] (accessed January 14, 2008).

[3] Ted Striphas, *The Late Age of Print: Everyday Book Culture from Consumerism to Control* (New York and London: Columbia University Press, 2009), 111–40; see also Cecelia Konchar Farr, *Reading Oprah: How Oprah's Book Club Changed the Way America Reads* (Albany, NY: State University of New York Press, 2005); Kathleen Rooney, *Reading With Oprah: The Book Club That Changed America* (Fayetteville, AR: University of Arkansas Press, 2005).

[4] Hereafter I refer to "Ian" without quotation marks and as a "he," recognizing that this internet handle may not properly identify her or him by name or sex.

[5] Ian, "Amazon Has Banned My Account—My Kindle Is Now a (Partial) Brick," *Mobile-Read* (April 6, 2009), http://www.mobileread.com/forums/showthread.php?t=44350&highlight=amazon+banning, post #1 (accessed July 4, 2009).

[6] Ibid., post #16.

[7] Joseph Turow, *Niche Envy: Marketing Discrimination in the Digital Age* (Cambridge, MA and London: MIT Press, 2006), 96.

[8] Ian, "Amazon Has Banned My Account," post #16.

[9] Ibid., post #77. Note that the consumer advocacy website *The Consumerist* picked up on and publicized Ian's story. This may have had something to do with Amazon.com's decision to reinstate his account. Chris Walters, "Amazon Can Ban You From Your Kindle Account Whenever it Likes," *The Consumerist* (April 15, 2009), http://consumerist.com/5213774/amazon-can-ban-you-from-your-kindle-account-whenever-it-likes.

[10] Jonathan Zittrain, *The Future of the Internet—and How to Stop It* (New Haven, CT and London: Yale University Press, 2008), 106; emphasis in original.

[11] Thomas Z. Freedman, *A Kindle in Every Backpack: A Proposal for eTextbooks in American Schools*, White Paper (Washington, DC: Democratic Leadership Council, 2009), http://www.dlc.org/documents/DLC_Freedman_Kindle_0709.pdf (accessed July 15, 2009); Jeffrey R. Young, "This Could Be the Year of e-Textbooks," *Chronicle of Higher Education* (September 11, 2009), A1, A12.

[12] Raymond Williams, "Culture and Technology," in *The Politics of Modernism: Against the New Conformists* (London and New York: Verso, 1989), 134.

[13] Alberto Manguel, *A History of Reading* (New York: Penguin Books, 1996), 67.

[14] C.f.: David M. Henkin, *City Reading: Written Words and Public Spaces in Antebellum New York* (New York: Columbia University Press, 1998).

[15] See, e.g., Lucien Febvre and Henri-Jean Martin, *The Coming of the Book: The Impact of Printing, 1450–1800*, trans. David Gerard (London and New York: Verso, 1976); Marshall McLuhan, *The Gutenberg Galaxy: The Making of Typographic Man* (Toronto: University of Toronto Press, 1962); Elizabeth L. Eisenstein, *The Printing Press as an Agent of Change: Communications and Cultural Transformations in Early-Modern Europe* (Cambridge: Cambridge University Press, 1979); Walter J. Ong, *Orality and Literacy: The Technologizing of the Word* (London and New York: Routledge, 1982); Adrian Johns, *The Nature of the Book:*

Print and Knowledge in the Making (Chicago and London: University of Chicago Press, 1998).

[16] Striphas, *Late Age of Print*, 23–6.
[17] Quoted in Levy, "Future of Reading," 57.
[18] "Jeff Bezos Interview," n.p.
[19] The phrase "paradox of the e-book" is an homage to James Carey, "The Paradox of the Book," *Library Trends* 33 (1984): 103–13.
[20] The packaging for Kindle's successors, Kindle 2 and the larger Kindle DX, has been streamlined. The bulky white codex has been replaced with a more modest brown box, although the inner wrapping preserves the cascading typography aesthetic of the original. The leather folio is an optional accessory on the newer models.
[21] Gerard Genette, *Paratexts: Thresholds of Interpretation*, trans. J.E. Lewin (Cambridge: Cambridge University Press, 1997).
[22] Levy, "The Future of Reading," 57. Note that the second generation Kindles—Kindle 2 and the Kindle DX—are thinner and lighter. Both, however, continue to be compared with ink-on-paper referents in Amazon's promotional materials. See, e.g., http://www.amazon.com/Kindle-Amazons-Wireless-Reading-Generation/dp/B00154JDAI/ref=amb_link_84549771_1?pf_rd_m=ATVPDKIKX0DER&pf_rd_s=center-1&pf_rd_r=045P15HANREDG818MK8R&pf_rd_t=101&pf_rd_p=482492931&pf_rd_i=507846; and http://www.amazon.com/Kindle-DX-Amazons-Wireless-Generation/dp/B0015TCML0/ref=kin2w_ddp (both websites accessed July 15, 2009).
[23] Quoted in Levy, "Future of Reading," 60; c.f. Nicholson Baker, "A New Page: Can the Kindle Really Improve on the Book?" *The New Yorker* (August 3, 2009): 25.
[24] Jeff Bezos, quoted in "Oprah's Favorite New Gadget," http://www.oprah.com/slideshow/oprahshow/20081024_tows_kindle/3 (accessed July 4, 2009).
[25] Michael Arrington, "Amazon May Sell $750 Million In Kindles by 2010 (That's A Lot Of Kindles)," *TechCrunch* (May 14, 2008), http://www.techcrunch.com/2008/05/14/amazon-may-sell-750-million-in-kindles-by-2010-thats-a-lot-of-kindles/ (accessed July 5, 2009); Erick Schonfeld, "We Know How Many Kindles Amazon Has Sold: 240,000," *TechCrunch* (August 1, 2008), http://www.techcrunch.com/2008/08/01/we-know-how-many-kindles-amazon-has-sold-240000/ (accessed July 5, 2009); Erick Schonfeld, "Those Kindle Estimates Keep Going Up," *TechCrunch* (August 11, 2008), http://www.techcrunch.com/2008/08/11/those-kindle-estimates-keep-going-up/ (accessed July 5, 2009); Michael Arrington, "Three Million Kindles Sold, Apparently," *TechCruch* (January 29, 2010), http://techcrunch.com/2010/01/29/3-million-amazon-kindles-sold-apparently/?utm_source=feedburner&utm_medium=feed&utm_campaign=Feed%3A+Techcrunch+%28TechCrunch%29&utm_content=Netvibes (accessed February 17, 2010).
[26] Gary Hall, *Digitize This Book! The Politics of New Media, or Why We Need Open Access Now* (Minneapolis and London: University of Minnesota Press, 2008), 59.
[27] Plato, *The Phaedrus: Compiled With an Introduction and Commentary by R. Hackforth* (Cambridge: Cambridge University Press, 1972), 156–64; see also Martin Heidegger, *Parmenides*, trans. André Schuwer and Richard Rojcewicz (Bloomington, IN: Indiana University Press, 1992), 81; Ong, *Orality and Literacy*; Birkerts, *The Gutenberg Elegies: The Fate of Reading in an Electronic Age* (New York: Fawcett Columbine, 1994); c.f. Jonathan Sterne, *The Audible Past: Cultural Origins of Sound Reproduction* (Durham, NC and London: Duke University Press, 2009), 215–86; Striphas, *Late Age of Print*, 23–6.
[28] Ong, *Orality and Literacy*, 12.
[29] Quoted in Levy, "Future of Reading," 58.
[30] "Amazon Kindle: License Agreement and Terms of Use," http://www.amazon.com/gp/help/customer/display.html?ie=UTF8&nodeId=200144530 (accessed July 5, 2009).
[31] "Amazon.com Privacy Notice," http://www.amazon.com/gp/help/customer/display.html?nodeId=468496 (accessed July 5, 2009).

[32] Alan Sipress, "At Web 2.0 Summit, a Look at What's in Store (and Storage)," *The Washington Post* (November 9, 2006), D1, http://www.washingtonpost.com/wp-dyn/content/article/2006/11/08/AR2006110802094.html (accessed October 4, 2008); Kevin Maney, "Amazon's New Direction: Point, Click, Make a Product to Sell to the World," *USA Today* (November 21, 2006), n.p., http://www.usatoday.com/tech/columnist/kevinmaney/2006-11-21-amazon-user-generated-products_x.htm (accessed October 4, 2008); Spence Reiss, "Cloud Computing. Available at Amazon.com Today," *Wired* (April 21, 2008), n.p., http://www.wired.com/techbiz/it/magazine/16-05/mf_amazon (accessed October 4, 2008); Nicholas Carr, *The Big Switch: Rewiring the World, From Edison to Google* (New York and London: W.W. Norton & Co., 2008): 72–5; c.f. Wade Roush, "Servers for Hire," *Technology Review* (September 28, 2006), http://www.technologyreview.com/business/17554/ (accessed July 22, 2009). There Amazon CEO Bezos states that its Web Services unit "is a completely separate business that will grow up in its own way."

[33] Carr, *Big Switch*, 74.

[34] Ibid., *passim*.

[35] "Amazon Web Services," http://aws.amazon.com/; "Amazon Elastic Compute Cloud (Amazon EC2)," http://aws.amazon.com/ec2/; "Amazon Simple Storage Service (Amazon S3)," http://aws.amazon.com/s3/; "Amazon SimpleDB," http://aws.amazon.com/simpledb/; "Amazon CloudFront," http://aws.amazon.com/cloudfront/ (all websites accessed July 22, 2009).

[36] Sarah Mahoney, "Keeping Amazon in Check: Consumers Plucking Up the Fruits of Bezos' Labor, But Privacy Crusaders Are on the Prowl," *Advertising Age* (June 1, 2005): n.p., Lexis-Nexis (accessed February 21, 2009).

[37] Robert D. Hof, "Jeff Bezos' Risky Bet," *Business Week* (November 13, 2006), http://www.businessweek.com/magazine/content/06_46/b4009001.htm (accessed October 4, 2008); see also Martin LaMonica, "Amazon: Utility Computing Power Broker," *CNET News* (November 16, 2006), http://news.cnet.com/Amazon-Utility-computing-power-broker/2100-7345_3-6135977.html (accessed October 4, 2008); Fred Vogelstein, "Great Wall of Facebook: The Social Network's Plan to Dominate the Internet—and Keep Google Out," *Wired* (June 22, 2009), http://www.wired.com/techbiz/it/magazine/17-07/ff_facebook-wall (accessed June 30, 2009); Fred Vogelstein, "The *Wired* Interview: Facebook's Mark Zuckerberg," *Wired* (June 29, 2009), http://www.wired.com/epicenter/2009/06/mark-zuckerberg-speaks/ (accessed June 30, 2009); Carr, *Big Switch*, 72–5.

[38] Eric Engleman, "Amazon.com: Don't Blame Us for Twitter Problems," *TechFlash* (April 7, 2009), http://www.techflash.com/Amazon_Dont_blame_us_for_Twitter_problems_42620667.html (accessed June 30, 2009); "Linden Lab (*Second Life*)," http://aws.amazon.com/solutions/case-studies/linden-lab/ (accessed June 30, 2009); Carr, *Big Switch*, 115; Chuck Salter, "#2 Amazon," *Fast Company* (February 17, 2010), http://www.fastcompany.com/mic/2010/profile/amazon (accessed February 18, 2010).

[39] "Amazon's Hot New Item: Its Data Center," *Forbes* (February 2, 2008), http://www.forbes.com/markets/feeds/afx/2008/02/02/afx4606529.html (accessed October 4, 2008).

[40] Oscar Gandy, "It's Discrimination, Stupid!" in *Resisting the Virtual Life: The Culture and Politics of Information*, ed. James Brooks and Iain A. Boal (San Francisco: City Lights Books, 1995), 39.

[41] Tiziana Terranova, *Network Culture: Politics for the Information Age* (London and Ann Arbor, MI: Pluto Press, 2004): 73–97; c.f. Pierre Lévy, *Collective Intelligence: Mankind's Emerging World in Cyberspace*, trans. Robert Bononno (Cambridge: Perseus Books, 1997); Henry Jenkins, *Convergence Culture: Where Old and New Media Collide* (New York and London: New York University Press, 2006).

[42] "In accounting terms, goodwill is described merely as the market price of an enterprise above and beyond that of the fair market value of its tangible assets (i.e. real estate, buildings, inventory, cash, credit, etc.) less its liabilities." Andrew Herman, Rosemary J. Coombe, and

[43] Lewis Kaye, "Your Second Life? Goodwill and the Performativity of Intellectual Property in Online Digital Gaming," *Cultural Studies* 20 (2006): 186.

[43] On the paradoxes of estranged labor, see Terranova, *Network Culture*, 75–80. See also Karl Marx, "Economic and Philosophic Manuscripts of 1844," in *The Marx-Engels Reader*, 2nd ed., ed. Robert C. Tucker (New York: W.W. Norton & Co., 1978), 70–81.

[44] Daniel J. Solove, *The Digital Person: Technology and Privacy in the Information Age* (New York and London: New York University Press, 2004), 89.

[45] On the embodied dimensions of reading, see: Carolyn Marvin, "The Body of the Text: Literacy's Corporeal Constant," *Quarterly Journal of Speech* 80 (1994): 129–49; Carolyn Marvin, "Bodies, Texts, and the Social Order: A Reply to Bielefeldt," *Quarterly Journal of Speech* 81 (1995): 103–7; Daniel Heller-Roazen, *Echolalias: On the Forgetting of Language* (New York: Zone Books, 2005); and Manguel, *History of Reading*, 45. On reading's cognitive dimensions, see McLuhan, *Gutenberg Galaxy*; and Ong, *Orality and Literacy*.

[46] *Amazon Mechanical Turk*, https://www.mturk.com/mturk/welcome (accessed August 28, 2009); Carr, *Big Switch*, 218–19; Hof, "Bezos' Risky Bet," n.p.

[47] "Overview > FAQ," *Amazon Mechanical Turk*, at https://www.mturk.com/mturk/help?helpPage=overview (accessed August 28, 2009).

[48] Adam Greenfield, *Everyware: The Dawning Age of Ubiquitous Computing* (Berkeley, CA: New Riders, 2006), 24.

[49] J.S. Mill, *On Liberty*, ed. Elizabeth Rapaport (Indianapolis, IN and Cambridge: Hackett Publishing Co., Inc., 1978), 11.

[50] Quoted in Azar Nafisi, *Reading Lolita in Tehran: A Memoir in Books* (New York: Random House, 2004), 19.

[51] Birkerts, *Gutenberg Elegies*, 87.

[52] Elizabeth Long, "Textual Interpretation as Collective Action," in *The Ethnography of Reading*, ed. Jonathan Boyarin (Berkeley: University of California Press, 1992), 184–93.

[53] Manguel, *History of Reading*, 51.

[54] Alexander R. Galloway, *Gaming: Essays on Algorithmic Culture* (Minneapolis and London: University of Minnesota Press, 2006); see also Solove, *Digital Person*, 49.

[55] Solove, *Digital Person*, 42, 19.

[56] "Privacy Notice," *Amazon.com*, http://www.amazon.com/gp/help/customer/display.html?nodeId=468496 (accessed September 7, 2009).

[57] Solove, *Digital Person*, 53; see also 51–5.

[58] Ibid., 83, 92.

[59] See, e.g., "Amazon Acquisitions and Investments," *Meet the Boss*, http://www.meettheboss.com/Images/amazon-acquisitions.png (accessed September 8, 2009).

[60] Solove, *Digital Person*, 203.

[61] Ibid., 202–3.

[62] "Privacy Notice," n. p.

[63] Solove, *Digital Person*, 204–5.

[64] David Pogue, "Some E-books Are More Equal Than Others," *Pogue's Posts/The New York Times* (July 17, 2009), http://pogue.blogs.nytimes.com/2009/07/17/some-e-books-are-more-equal-than-others/ (accessed September 11, 2009); Brad Stone, "Amazon Erases Orwell Books From Kindle," *The New York Times* (July 18, 2009), http://www.nytimes.com/2009/07/18/technology/companies/18amazon.html (accessed September 11, 2009); *Justin Gawronski and Antoine Bruguier v. Amazon.com, Inc. and Amazon Digital Services, Inc.* Plaintiffs' Complaint, U.S.D.C. (W.D.W.) 2009, http://www.scribd.com/doc/17956203/Amazon-Class-Action-Lawsuit-Filing (accessed August 15, 2009); Geoffrey A. Fowler, "Lawsuit: Amazon Ate My Homework," *The Wall Street Journal* (July 30, 2009), http://blogs.wsj.com/digits/2009/07/30/lawsuit-amazon-ate-my-homework/ (accessed September 11, 2009); Tim Klass, "High School Student Sues Amazon Over Orwell," *MSNBC* (July 31, 2009),

http://www.msnbc.msn.com/id/32236930/ns/technology_and_science-tech_and_gadgets/ (accessed September 11, 2009).

[65] Jeffrey P. Bezos, "An Apology From Amazon," *Kindle Community* (July 23, 2009), http://www.amazon.com/tag/kindle/forum/?_encoding=UTF8&cdForum=Fx1D7SY3BVSESG&cdMsgNo=1&cdPage=1&cdSort=oldest&cdThread=Tx1FXQPSF67X1IU&displayType=tagsDetail&cdMsgID=Mx2G7WLMRCU49NO#Mx2G7WLMRCU49NO&tag=kwab-20 (accessed July 24, 2009).

[66] *Justin Gawronski and Antoine Bruguier v. Amazon.com, Inc. and Amazon Digital Services, Inc*; Miguel Helft, "Amazon.com Offers to Replace Copies of Orwell Book," *The New York Times* (September 4, 2009), http://www.nytimes.com/2009/09/05/technology/companies/05amazon.html (accessed September 10, 2009); Eric Engleman, "Amazon Settles Lawsuit Over Deleted Copy of '1984,'" *TechFlash* (September 30, 2009), http://www.techflash.com/seattle/2009/09/amazon_settles_lawsuit_over_deleted_1984.html (accessed February 17, 2010).

[67] Aeschalus, *Prometheus Bound* and *Seven Against Thebes,* trans. Theodore Alois Buckley (Philadelphia, PA: David McKay, 1897/Project Gutenberg, 2008), e-book; Levy, "Future of Reading," 57.

[68] "Plastic Logic eReader Will Wirelessly Connect Using AT&T 3G Network," *Plastic Logic* (July 22, 2009), press release, http://www.plasticlogic.com/news/prReaderWirelesslyConnectATTJul222009.php (accessed September 15, 2009); Priya Ganapati, "Sony's E-Book Reader Adds Touchscreen, Wireless Downloads," *Wired* (August 25, 2009), http://www.wired.com/gadgetlab/2009/08/sony-wireless-reader/ (accessed September 15, 2009).

[69] As Cory Doctorow wrote upon learning of the Amazon/*1984* incident: "Amazon claims that they won't do this again. But as every good novelist knows, 'A gun on the mantlepiece [sic] in act one must go off by act three.' Once it's possible for the mothership to remotely zap all our devices, the possibility exists that a hacker will attack them, or a courtroom will order an injunction against them (at one point, a US magistrate ordered ReplayTV to send out a firmware update that would brick its devices as part of the preliminaries to a court case), or the feature will go haywire, or the management of Amazon will change." Cory Doctorow, "Amazon's Orwellian Deletion of Kindle Books," *BoingBoing* (July 20, 2009), http://www.boingboing.net/2009/07/20/amazons-orwellian-de.html (accessed September 15, 2009).

[70] Michael E. Gardiner, *Critiques of Everyday Life* (London and New York: Routledge, 2000): 107.

[71] "What Is the Commodity Here?" *Differences and Repetitions Wiki,* comment, http://striphas.wikidot.com/kindle-the-labor-of-reading-worksite/comments/show#post-283003 (accessed September 15, 2009).

[72] On tactics, see Michel de Certeau, *The Practice of Everyday Life,* trans. Stephen Rendall (Berkeley: University of California Press, 1984), xvii–xx.

[73] Isaiah Berlin, "Two Concepts of Liberty," http://www.nyu.edu/projects/nissenbaum/papers/twoconcepts.pdf (accessed January 4, 2009), published originally in *Four Essays on Liberty* (Oxford: Oxford University Press, 1958), 118–72.

[74] Lawrence Grossberg, "Does Cultural Studies Have Futures? Should it? (Or, What's the Matter With New York?), *Cultural Studies* 20 (2006): 1–32; Ted Striphas, "Harry Potter and the Simulacrum: Contested Copies in an Age of Intellectual Property," *Critical Studies in Media Communication* 26 (2009): 295–311; see also Yochai Benkler, *The Wealth of Networks: How Social Production Transforms Markets and Freedom* (New Haven, CT and London: Yale University Press, 2006): esp. 273–300; Lawrence Lessig, *Remix: Making Art and Commerce Thrive in the Hybrid Economy* (New York: Penguin, 2008).

[75] Michael Warner, *The Letters of the Republic: Publication and the Public Sphere in Eighteenth-Century America* (Cambridge, MA and London: Harvard University Press, 1990), esp. 118–50.

[76] Julie E. Cohen, "A Right to Read Anonymously: A Close Look at 'Copyright Management' in Cyberspace," *Connecticut Law Review* 28 (1996): 981–1039; see also Jessica Litman, "The

Exclusive Right to Read," *Cardozo Arts and Entertainment Law Journal* 13 (1994): 29–54; and Richard Stallman, "The Right to Read," *Communications of the ACM* 40 (1997): 85–7.

[77] Cohen, "Right to Read Anonymously," 1006; emphasis in original.
[78] Ibid., 1013.
[79] Ibid., 1010.
[80] Ibid., 1011.
[81] You cannot, for example, share or resell a Kindle title once you have finished reading it, as you might do with a printed book. On technological protection measures, see Kristin R. Eschenfelder; "Every Library's Nightmare? Digitial Rights Management, Use Restrictions, and Licensed Scholarly Digital Resources," *College and Research Libraries* 69 (2008): 205–23; on the tightening of intellectual property laws, see Litman, "Exclusive Right to Read."
[82] Lessig, *Remix*, 23–114.
[83] Lawrence Lessig, *Free Culture: How Big Media Uses Technology and the Law to Lock Down Culture and Control Creativity* (New York: Penguin Press, 2004), 218; Kembrew McLeod, *Freedom of Expression®: Overzealous Copyright Bozos and Other Enemies of Creativity* (New York: Doubleday, 2005), 29; Tarleton Gillespie, *Wired Shut: Copyright and the Shape of Digital Culture* (Cambridge, MA and London: MIT Press, 2007), 197.
[84] Cohen, "Right to Read Anonymously," 1037; c.f. Jessica Litman, who states: "What the public needs is a copyright lawyer of its own to represent it." Litman, "Excusive Right to Read," 53.

The Postcolonial Predicament of Gay Rights in the *Queen Boat* Affair

Julian Awwad

The Queen Boat 52 *is the most highly-publicized crackdown on same-sex practices in an Arab country. By examining the case, this paper intervenes into the recent debate on gay rights activism in Arab and Islamic countries and addresses the postcolonial predicament facing human rights activists on the question of intervention. The paper proposes to reconcile the tension between critiques of gay rights activism and the practical imperative to address state violations against same-sex practitioners. Because the state bases its persecution of homosexuals on the constitution of gay subjectivity, the paper argues that Egypt's postcolonial condition, like that of other Arab countries, necessitates a human rights framework that is based on a discourse and a set of strategies for attaining sexual rights that activists cannot not want to employ.*

On May 11, 2001, the police descended upon the *Queen Boat*, a neon-lit tourist boat moored on the Nile in Cairo and a floating discotheque that was informally known to be a hang-out for allegedly gay men. The police rounded up the men, who were almost exclusively Egyptian, loaded them into state security vehicles, and hauled them off to El Azbakiyya police station in downtown Cairo. Thirty-five men were arrested, as well as seventeen others from elsewhere, off the streets of Cairo, all of whom constituted the iconic *Queen Boat 52*. All of the detained were tortured and subjected to invasive and humiliating forensic examinations.[1] Abuse of the detainees continued in the Egyptian media, which heavily covered the case especially during the early stages, and extended to the detainees' families. That the case involved religious beliefs and morality ensured the public's engagement.[2]

On July 18, 2001, the *Queen Boat* trial began in an Emergency State Security Court,[3] and on November 14, 2001, twenty-three of the fifty-two men were sentenced to prison. The remaining twenty-nine defendants were acquitted. After the men had spent one year in prison, in late May 2002, President Mubarak rescinded the verdicts of the trial except for the two men who were convicted on the charge of "contempt of religion," holding that the charges of "habitual debauchery" should not have been heard in the State Security Court.[4] One month later, however, the files of the acquitted men were referred to the state prosecution service for review, and they were tried again in the Court of Misdemeanors in July 2002.[5] Again, the men were found guilty of the same crime and, following some appeals, the verdict was upheld; although, sentences were reduced by one year.[6]

The *Queen Boat 52* case remains the most highly-publicized crackdown on same-sex practices in an Arab country. The plight of the accused received much international attention and substantial commentary, both of which seized the example of the case to make pronouncements on the overall situation of same-sex practices in Arab and Islamic countries. Taking its cues from the *Queen Boat* affair, this paper aims to reconcile the impetus for human rights interventions, namely in cases involving gay rights in the Arab and Islamic regions, and recent critical engagements with these interventions, especially in light of Joseph Massad's argument against what he calls the "Gay International." Whereas human rights work is compelled by the imperative to address state violations against same-sex practitioners, such intervention presumes and produces, according to Massad, homosexuals and gays where they do not exist. A postcolonial predicament emerges for human rights work: intervention is problematic because it adopts a universalizing posture and non-intervention overlooks the plight of persecuted same-sex practitioners and renders the state unaccountable for its violations. This predicament reveals a tension between critiques of gay rights activism and the practical imperative to address state violations against same-sex practitioners.

How to address this predicament is the issue that this paper raises. The paper begins by establishing that the Egyptian state relies on the constitution of gay subjectivity to justify its persecution of same-sex practitioners. This constitution is informed by Egypt's postcolonial condition, which, in turn, has increasingly become informed by the exigencies of neoliberal globalization. Because protections under the Egyptian Constitution are currently suspended under emergency law, Egypt's postcoloniality in an era of globalization becomes relevant for going beyond the instrumentality of the law to identify the ways in which Egyptian cultural norms contributed to the legal constitution of gay subjectivity. Consequently, how to conceive the plight of homosexuals *after* the state is prompted to will them to exist is the question that the postcolonial predicament raises. Egypt's postcolonial condition, like that of other Arab countries, necessitates a human rights framework that is based on a discourse and strategies for attaining sexual rights that activists *cannot not* want

Sexuality and the Afterlife of Colonialism

Although Egyptian law does not expressly criminalize same-sex acts, the constitution of the homosexual as a subject at law was necessary. In other words, the Egyptian government was compelled to legally constitute gay subjectivity. This impulse represents a curiously interesting historical moment that engages Egypt's postcoloniality in two ways. First, the *Queen Boat* case and the struggle to abolish prostitution during the last days of colonial rule convene around the same law. The creatively interpreted law combating prostitution under which the defendants were charged had been drafted in the heydays of nationalist struggle "as a response to what was viewed as a remnant of Egypt's colonial past."[7] Upon occupying Egypt in 1882, the British had set out to regulate legalized prostitution rather than outlawing it in accordance with Christian colonial moralizing evident elsewhere in the Empire.[8] The legalization of prostitution was primarily maintained for the benefit of European settlers and soldiers and remained vital in Egyptian urban life throughout British rule.[9] Egyptian nationalists, including well-known feminists such as Huda Sha'rawi, seized upon the legal trade in prostitution as an example of the social ills symptomatic of British occupation, and combating licensed brothels became an issue of patriotism and national honor.[10] The abolishment of prostitution became concomitant to decolonization, especially for Islamic nationalists who viewed the abolishment of prostitution as "a rejection of the promiscuity of alien sexual culture, and the purging of alien sex workers from Egypt's urban spaces."[11]

Second, the *Queen Boat* case and the struggle to abolish prostitution convene around the same set of conceptual as well as circumstantial predicates. The law combating prostitution did not take effect until 1951,[12] some twenty years after independence, presumably because of the presence of allied troops in Egypt during the Second World War.[13] Conceptually, prostitution was linked to foreign occupation and influence inasmuch as same-sex practices, especially in the *Queen Boat* case, are perceived as a Western imposition, or, at least, as a sign of Western influence.[14] It is constructed as a lurid and immediate threat that "colonizes" local subjects and infiltrates into an otherwise presumably-reclaimed "pure" or "authentic" society.

The struggle for reclaiming authenticity has historically been bound with nationalist struggles against imperial forces in the era of decolonization, especially where sexuality is involved. The historical circumstances in both these cases reveal an all too familiar pattern. Curiously, El Azbakiyya police station is a common scene in the historical plot which repeatedly concerns the enforcement of laws dealing with "scandalous public acts."[15] The battle of reclaiming sovereignty also requires the exception of non-Egyptians from the national "authenticating" process, as is evident under the Capitulations of the early twentieth century[16] as well as the pointed release of foreign nationals and women who were amongst the Egyptian men rounded up during the arrests.[17] This exception ejects the foreign elements from the body politic upon which the state assumes its sovereignty and its legal jurisdiction is cast. Egyptian public reaction was additionally reinforced against the United States and governments of the European Union when they implicated foreign aid and trade agreements in their defense of the plight of the detainees.[18]

Gay Subjectivity in an Era of Globalization

In the absence of legal prohibitions on homosexuality, why and how a gay legal subjectivity is constituted becomes relevant. Egyptian postcoloniality informs two important historical concerns that have had a significant effect on the government's approach to prostitution after independence, and, more recently, homosexual conduct in the *Queen Boat 52*: "anti-imperialist Egyptian nationalism articulated as sexual purity, and the secular state defending itself against the growing power of the Muslim Brotherhood."[19] Indeed, sexual purity as moral conduct is the requisite upon which the Egyptian secular state congeals with Islam in articulating a "virtuous" nationalism against the backdrop of economic uncertainty. Several observers argued that the main motive for staging the *Queen Boat 52* is to divert public attention from the economic woes of the country and the effects of economic liberalization, including increasing poverty especially among the youth.[20] This diversion took place in the context of an ongoing economic crisis after Egypt adopted neoliberal economic reforms to secure international aid for national development, resulting in the privatization of the public sector and the dismantling of social welfare mechanisms.[21]

The impact of these socioeconomic difficulties on gender roles is unmistakable. Legislation enshrines gender norms: "whereby men are seen as the main providers and protectors of the family, whilst women are cast as mothers and wives, whose primary sphere of activity is the home."[22] Consequently, economic instability resulted in patriarchal instability: women's status and visibility in the public sphere became connected to national modernity in addition to the demands of international economic institutions.[23] In a context of scarce economic opportunities and the allocation of resources towards women's initiatives, men's anxieties about their sexuality within a framework of changing gender relations were exacerbated.[24] One interpretation of the *Queen Boat* incident follows that it is "an attempt to punish homosexuality in order to 'rescue' Egyptian masculinity from the insecurities experienced as a result of socioeconomic changes and shifting gender roles. Continued masculine domination depends upon the maintenance of heteronormativity—that is, the institutionalization of heterosexuality as the norm within society."[25] Women's rights as a symbol of national modernity and a challenge to patriarchal masculinity became concomitant with anxieties over the proper sexual conduct of the nation's men.

It is this new crisis of postcolonial modernity over which sovereignty is claimed and external (economic) domination is at least diffused, although not overcome, by displacing economic anxieties onto the moral conduct of the nation. Partha Chatterjee's distinction between the "inner," or spiritual, and the "outer," or material, domains created by anticolonial nationalism serves to conceptualize postcolonial sovereignty in an age of global capitalism; or, how the "globalization of perversion"—as it was perceived in the Egyptian press[26]— is derivative from the globalization of capital:

> The material is the domain of the "outside," of the economy and of statecraft, of science and technology, a domain where the West had proved its superiority and the East had succumbed. In this domain, then, Western superiority had to be acknowledged and its accomplishments carefully studied and replicated. The spiritual, on the other hand, is an "inner" domain bearing the "essential" marks of cultural identity. The greater one's success in imitating Western skills in the material domain, therefore, the greater the need to preserve the distinctness of one's spiritual culture.[27]

Chatterjee furthermore argues that anitcolonial nationalism creates its domain of sovereignty within colonial society well before political battles with the colonial powers actually begin.[28] In a similar vein, the assertion of Egyptian sovereignty in the *Queen Boat* case occurred well before the political battles which subsequently ensued.[29]

The similarities between the abolition of prostitution in colonial Egypt and attempts to combat homosexuality are testament to this struggle for sovereignty. The *Queen Boat* case was, indeed, the first time that the Egyptian state had publicly and formally recognized the existence of homosexuals as a group or community. Their presence was depicted to conjure images of threatening "networks," "organizations," and "cults" to be feared.[30] While the outer domain of nationalism relinquishes sovereignty to Western economic superiority and exigencies of economic liberalization, the state turns to its inner domain for compensation. Same-sex practitioners become the "homo sacers," to use Giorgio Agamben's term, as biopolitical subjects of the Egyptian state upon whom the state can assert jurisdiction to establish its sovereignty.[31]

Egyptian nationalism is, moreover, orchestrated by deploying a discourse of religiosity. Homosexual acts as affronts to the "heavenly religions" and to nature have been so characterized, as sinful and abnormal, by many representatives of the Egyptian state.[32] This deployment is imperative should the Egyptian secular government want to maintain the moral high ground against the increasing popularity of the Islamists. The popularity of the Muslim Brotherhood in the 1940s and 1950s may well explain the final enactment of the law on combating prostitution. Similarly, the recent political gains of the Muslim Brotherhood provided ample incentive for the government to promote its image as guardian of public virtue. In order to deflate the fledgling Islamist opposition movement, the persecution of the Islamist threat had to be combined with actions that bolstered the state's religiosity and "Islamic credentials."[33]

The popularity of the Muslim Brotherhood is complemented by Egypt's newfound religiosity. The group's concern and proven record on social issues have won the Islamists a sizable presence in the Egyptian parliament, after the Egyptian government allowed multi-party elections to encourage democratization. The Brotherhood's critical stance against the Mubarak government's handling of the economy and against the government's secular outlook as the source for this mishandling corresponds to the group's newfound political legitimacy.[34] Consequently, the *Queen Boat* became the means onto which needed economic and political reforms have been displaced in a manner that would not only bolster the government's Islamic credentials but would ensure that its "policy of distraction"[35] captured the fascination of the Egyptian public at large, the Islamists included.

The Urgency of "Cultural Constitutions"

The Egyptian Constitution enshrines rights and protections for individual citizens. It is one that appears to comply with basic notions of human rights and freedoms.[36] Even a cursory glance at chapter 3 of the Constitution entitled "Public Freedoms, Rights and Duties" reveals an express commitment to the equality of all citizens (article 40); the conducting of arrests and detention in accordance with the preservation of human dignity without moral or physical harm (article 42); the protection of the inviolability of an individual's privacy (article 45); and the criminalization of any assault on individual freedom or on the inviolability of privacy and other public rights and liberties (article 57).

Nevertheless, the Egyptian Constitution also reveals the secular government's relationship to religion. The Constitution, as a reflection of the values and norms of Egyptian society, depicts a picture in which religion is a central source for prescribing these values. Article 2 stipulates Islam as the religion of the state, and Islamic jurisprudence (shari'a law) as the principal source of legislation. The centrality of religion is furthermore evident in the manner in which it is guaranteed to inform the constituent elements of society as well as moral and national values. Article 9 establishes the family as the basis of society construed according to religion, morality, and patriotism, and article 11 recognizes women's role and equality in society; although this role is nevertheless informed by a woman's duty to her family as prescribed by the rules of Islamic jurisprudence (shari'a). As if to leave no room for equivocation, article 19 emphatically instructs the centrality of religion and the manner in which it informs the lives of citizens by formally-maintaining religious education as a principal subject to be taught.

The values and identity of the nation, as they are represented in the text of the Egyptian Constitution, can be understood as an ongoing process of constant revelation. The Constitution does not simply reveal what the Egyptian nation *is*. As a cultural text, the Constitution engages at least two conceptions of culture: broadly, in the sociological and anthropological senses, it is the lived experience or particular way of life of a group or people, and, narrowly, it is part of the practices of intellectual activity—broadly-construed—of a group or society.[37] Both conceptions inform the Constitution as a postcolonial, cultural artifact constituting the postcolonial nation.

It is useful to conceptualize the Egyptian Constitution according to this framework. The Constitution expressly espouses and produces the values and norms of Egyptian society. It also serves as a symbolic representation of Egyptian lived experience or "culture" in its broadest sense. Even though the Constitution was trumped by emergency laws, constitutional values that circumscribed the religious morality of Egyptian society were, nevertheless, invoked in the *Queen Boat* case. Consequently, only individuals who comport with the moral conduct of the nation are deemed deserving, in this cultural sense, of (constitutional) guarantees and protections. It is in this way that the integrity of the Constitution as a symbol of the lived culture of a moral Egyptian nation is vicariously restored.

Current religious interpretations of, and the stance against homosexuality, preclude the condoning of homosexual conduct as morally acceptable. Same-sex acts contravene social and religious mores and norms. Considering the colonial history of the law enacted to combat prostitution, the creative interpretation of "debauchery" (Arabic: *fujūr*) transformed the notion from "an instrument of moral condemnation rather than legal exactitude"[38] into a legal concept determinative of unlawful male sexual conduct. Yet, the human rights violations which took place during the *Queen Boat* case are jarring in contrast to the constitutionally-enshrined protections and guarantees of individual rights. These violations contradict claims that mechanisms, which have been established prior to the *Queen Boat* case, preserve the individual rights of Egyptian citizens in accordance with international instruments and notions of human rights, and, in doing so, hold the legislative and executive branches accountable to the Constitution.[39] Instead, the *Queen Boat* case demonstrates the flagrant bypass of the Constitution by the Egyptian government through its continued extension of emergency laws.

The legal justification for prosecuting the defendants in the *Queen Boat* case also required that same-sex conduct have ramifications for national security. As a social issue eliciting moral condemnation, the *legal* condemnation of homosexual conduct was possible through emergency laws which trumped constitutional protections in the context of a state of national emergency. Because a moral issue was made to engage national security in the public's view, the legal means through which the Egyptian government proceeded to recuperate the nation's morality were legitimized by a religiously informed public that neither had sympathies for homosexuality nor the imperative to discern the legality of such recuperation.

The foreclosure by legal means of any possibility for resorting to rights and guarantees under the Egyptian Constitution deemed those who may want to invoke them equally undeserving should they fall outside the cultural constitution of religious morality. By default, the state gains to benefit by tightening its political grip in the "inner domain" of the nation, wherein not only did it appear to be an equally effective guardian of religious values, as the Islamists, but sought to co-opt them into its campaign. The campaign against same-sex conduct was also deployed against religious fundamentalists who, in joining the chorus of moral admonition, effectively legitimized the means of legal redress in the very same courts used in their persecution, a testament to the state's power to co-opt adversaries.[40] Recourse to the Constitution would otherwise retain citizens' rights and protections under it, and constitutional guarantees would equally permit same-sex practitioners to live their lives as they had before. Through emergency laws, a simultaneous, paradoxical deployment of one set of constitutional values (religious and social values) disregarded another set (individual rights and freedoms) altogether through an urgent cultural constitution.

As a Western modality of the "outer domain" of international relations, the Egyptian Constitution is re-constituted culturally. The concept of constitution could be understood in at least two senses: the first refers to the composition, constituent parts and fundamental make-up of a society, of what it *is*; and the second, refers to the notion that it is active "doing," something that is made culturally through history.[41] Viewed from the lens of the *Queen Boat*, the practice of interpreting the Constitution engages both these notions. The effect of emergency state laws is to nurture an unholy complicity with a particular set of constitutional values. This complicity legally resulted in a culturally-based rendition of the constitution of the nation, of who Egyptians are, or—for those less fortunate to fall outside its constitution—ought to be. It instructs men on the proper manifestations of Egyptian citizenship. The effect of emergency laws is to inform not only the terms of men's membership in society but to *act* on the constitution of the nation itself.

Egyptian modernity is informed by, if not subjected to, the imperatives of the "outer domain," the Western-dominated domain of international affairs and the global economy. However, as individual rights and freedoms are rendered in favor of those individuals who morally merit their bestowal, it is ostensibly from within the "inner domain" of spiritual morality that such determinations are made. The defense of culture, against affronts to the cultural authenticity of the nation, has equally become an all too familiar, even predictable, reaction to issues that have more to do with the state's economic and political incapacities than with actual cultural threats. The effective legitimization of the authoritarian grip of the regime seems, in the *Queen Boat* case, to suspend the Egyptian nation into a permanent state of anxiety over its sovereignty.[42] Claims of cultural authenticity arguably exacerbate the postcolonial predicament by evoking the lineaments of the colonial past in the postcolonial present. These claims become the typical tune which articulates the clamor of modern anxieties.

Cultural Authenticity and the Epistemology of Gay Rights

When Joseph Massad published an article criticizing the role of international human rights organizations in universalizing the Western discourse of gay identity in Arab and Muslim countries,[43] he set off a controversy with grave implications for human rights work. In his article, Massad argues that, what he terms the Gay International, comprising of "missionary tasks, the discourse that produces them, and the organizations that represent them," embarked upon a mission "to liberate Arab and Muslim 'gays and lesbians' from the oppression under which they allegedly live by transforming them from practitioners of same-sex contact into subjects who identify as homosexual or gay."[44] Massad contends that contrary "to the liberatory claims made by the Gay International in relation to what it posits as an always already homosexualized population … it is the discourse of the Gay International that both produces homosexuals, as well as gays and lesbians, where they do not exist, and represses same-sex desires and practices that refuse to be assimilated into its sexual epistemology."[45] According to Massad, the Gay International seeks to fix the instability of Arab and Muslim sexual desire that has historically confounded Western understanding and has, as a result, been managed through Orientalist knowledge.[46]

It follows, then, that constituents of the Gay International, including Westernized and self-identified gay Arabs, intervened in the *Queen Boat* to achieve this stabilization of sexual desire. Like the Egyptian government, their interventions equally invoked tropes of cultural authenticity that underwrites the postcolonial logic upon which gay subjectivity is constituted. In postcolonial societies, the discursive battleground upon which supporters and opponents of gay rights fight their battles, it appears, is characterized by cultural authenticity as its leitmotif. Carl Stychin identifies two positions, the cultural nationalist and the postcolonial gay:

> The two positions interpret the history of colonialism and the authenticity of tradition, as well as colonialism's relationship to sexuality, differently. Both embrace, in competing ways "national identity" and "universal rights," yet each fails to recognize how the opposing position is intimately related to and constitutive of its own argument. That is, both positions prioritize the sexual in the construction of individual and national identity, and each position is constituted through an antagonistic relationship with the other.[47]

Stychin indicates that both positions ahistorically reinvent the past and provide romanticized accounts of traditional, pre-colonial culture: the cultural nationalist position invokes a stable, traditional heterosexual culture destroyed by the colonial encounter, and the postcolonial gay position celebrates the accommodation of diverse sexual activity despite Western-based categorical sexual identities.[48] Furthermore, this postcolonial reinvention of the past seems to rely on the orientalist method upon which representation of Arab and Muslim desires are constructed.[49] The heterosexual-homosexual binary, thus, informs the orientalist epistemology underlying the postcolonial logic to which both supporters and opponents of gay rights subscribe.

It is curious that what animates both groups is this orientalist epistemology, of a stable, pure, uncontaminated pre-colonial culture, despite the diverging reinvention of its history. However, as Stychin argues, "appeals to tradition provide at best a partial but often incomplete story and at worst a misreading of history in the service of current political struggles."[50] Brian Whitaker rightly points out to the entanglement of attitudes towards homosexuality and human rights in general in international politics.[51] As in other contexts, the *Queen Boat* affair demonstrates the attempt by the Egyptian state to appropriate Western norms of respectability and order and to consolidate national identity in the wake of economic globalization.[52] While in the colonial context, foreign elements were perceived from without the nation-state, it becomes incumbent upon the postcolony to constitute the foreign element from within. In this case, gay subjectivity is superimposed onto the bodies of individuals engaged in same-sex activities, sacrificial bodies, or "homo sacers," that are at once necessary for consolidating the sovereignty of the state and with whom the state cannot dispense."[53]

However, the orientalist method underwriting these attitudes towards homosexuality exacerbates the severity of the postcolonial predicament *vis-à-vis* gay rights. For example, Whitaker acknowledges that attitudes against homosexuality are closely linked to other political, social, religious, and cultural issues.[54] In arguing for sexual rights as a basic element of human rights in the context of Arab reform, Whitaker states that "[t]here is little hope of developing sexual rights except within a framework of broadly-based reform, and only when Arab societies start to debate sexuality in a *rational* way will it be possible to *regard them as serious* about reform in general."[55] The orientalist undertones of Whitaker's argument unmistakably resonate with the very postcolonial predicament of configuring gay rights as human rights in the context of Arab societies. He adopts a typical orientalist posture towards the presupposed irrationality of Arab societies. That colonial discourses have typically configured sexuality in irrational terms suggests that this argument characterizes Arab public discourse as frivolous. There is equally a danger in privileging gay rights in this manner as the measure for effective reform.

Nowhere does Whitaker question the epistemology upon which gay rights are claimed, and upon which his thesis rests, falling squarely within Massad's critique. Whereas Whitaker takes issue with Massad's criticism of the "orientalist impulse" of the human rights community, the crux of Whitaker's argument, as he states it, perhaps unwittingly, exhibits that very impulse. Whitaker responds as follows:

> There are plenty of reasons other than an "orientalist impulse" why gay rights activists might pay special attention to Muslim countries, however, Massad gives no hint that discrimination and abuses in Arab countries have anything to do with it ... The portrayal of Western campaigners as interfering busybodies might have more credibility if gay and lesbian Arabs were in a position to organise themselves in their own countries. On the whole, they are not. Consequently agitation from abroad, often with secret collaboration from anonymous people inside the country, has become a well-established practice.[56]

If Western human rights campaigners interfere because local organization is lacking, Whitaker fails to escape the "orientalist impulse," again, by justifying the manner of civilizing missions of colonialism past and the burden of Western human rights activism to save Arab homosexuals from the passivity of their oppressive position. In a similar vein, according to the orientalist method, as Massad points out, "Arabs and Muslims can only be objects of European scholarship and never its subjects or audience (the inclusion of native informants notwithstanding)."[57] It appears that, by the same token, and according to Whitaker, Arabs and Muslims can only be the object of human rights activism and organization and never its subjects. Still, as Whitaker himself rightly maintains, "[e]xposure to foreign ideas and influences cannot be prevented, but nor are Arabs incapable of making critical judgments about them. Equally, Arab culture cannot be treated as a fossil."[58] Yet, his analysis mistakenly attributes claims of cultural authenticity to cultural nationalists alone and remains bereft of any serious attention to Arab critical engagements with gay rights discourse.

Massad's critical engagement is but one example.

Whitaker seems to dismiss such critical engagements, and instead criticizes approaches that rely on invisibility, claiming that "[e]xperience with the development of sexual rights in other countries shows that it is only when people make a fuss, and have the necessary organisation to back it up, that conditions improve."[59] Yet he does not indicate which countries these might be nor does he reconcile the breadth of his statement with the differences he, nevertheless, curiously recognizes across Arab countries, especially in his discussion between the Lebanese and Egyptian approaches; their "native informant" status, according to Massad, notwithstanding.[60] How might he account for an Egyptian activist's skepticism in emphasizing visibility or his need to "explore non-Western ways of being gay?"[61] This sentiment resonates with El Menyawi's reassessment of visibility based activism which he believes provides the state with easy targets that are deployed "as a scapegoat for other problems such as rising unemployment and poverty."

Otherwise, a reliance on the language of gay identity and rights prompts the advocate to adopt a law-first approach and to instrumentally engage with the law. This approach privileges human rights law and the letter of the Egyptian Constitution. It implies a legal realism according to which the law's effectiveness is measured by the way in which it produces its intended or desired effect based on universal categories. It is in this vein that Massad argued that the "discourse [of the Gay International] assumes prediscursively that homosexuals, gays, and lesbians are universal categories that exist everywhere in the world, and based on this prediscursive axiom, the Gay International sets itself the mission of defending them by demanding that their rights as 'homosexuals' be granted where they are denied and be respected where they are violated."[62]

Consequently, the language of gay rights, as it appears in the visibility-based strategies and discourse of the Gay International incites the state to discourse, as Massad argues.[63] Massad contends that the state has been incited to adopt a Western-based discourse on homosexuality. He offers the "incitement" argument to explain why the state is prompted to persecute individuals who engage in same-sex practices.[64] As Carl Stychin points out, "Western categorical discourses of sexuality clearly do not apply universally. Cultural nationalists, however, mistakenly think they do and thus are caught in the logic of colonialism without realizing it."[65] Postcolonial gays, in addition, continue to adopt a universalizing posture regarding gay rights. Beholden to this postcolonial logic, both groups "overlook the effects of colonialist and capitalist power in managing the sexualities of *all its subjects*,"[66] becoming heterosexualized or homosexualized in the process.

Sexual Dissidence and the Question of Rights

Despite the intense discomfort and opposition that it generated, Massad's critique of the Gay International is nevertheless relevant to any reconsideration of human rights interventions where homosexuals or gays have been willfully made to exist—that is, through the dynamic complicity of the postcolonial logic exhibited in the discursive postures of both the Gay International and the postcolonial state. The *Queen Boat* affair is a case in point. Central to Massad's argument is the queer idea that same-sex contact and activity do not equate to homosexuality or gay identity as a categorical mode of social organization around the heterosexual–homosexual binary. It seems that many amongst his critics overlook this crucial point and embark upon a rebuttal that tacitly equates same-sex contact with identity-based homosexuality, without tackling this point head on.[67] What this failure demonstrates is a manifestation of Massad's very argument: that the epistemology of homosexuality is so entrenched in the minds of activists that same-sex contact *as* homosexuality or gay identity is an underlying assumption requiring no interrogation. For example, the report issued by Amnesty International embraces this assumption and unequivocally promotes the notion that sexual orientation is a fundamental aspect of identity.[68]

The epistemology of gay identity, moreover, has increasingly come to inform the discourse on sexuality in Arab societies as well. As Massad indicates, the advent of colonialism has generally influenced Arab and Islamic attitudes and language regarding sexuality.[69] For better or worse, it may come as no surprise that this influence, then, informs the epistemology of gay identity today. Massad's argument presumes that responsibility for incitement lies squarely with the constituents of the Gay International. His argument does not question what benefits the state might have in playing into this incitement in the manner that it does; that is, in a manner that conveniently adopts rather than rejects—as Massad's critique compels us to do—the epistemology of the Gay International. The state's vested interest in this epistemology appears to fall outside the scope of his examination. Indeed, what responsibility does the state have in subscribing to the discourse incited by the Gay International?

This question engages the place of human rights work in postcolonial societies and the practical strategies available for human rights activists *after* the state has been incited to will homosexuals and gays to exist. It is unclear what role and relevance there is for human rights work beyond, and in light of, Massad's critical intervention. His can be regarded as a categorical diagnosis of a problematic framework for gay rights activism with seemingly no remedial effects. How activists could get past this impasse by (re)conceptualizing the practical strategies that are required to address the plight of detainees, such as those in the *Queen Boat*, remains unaddressed. Once gay subjectivity has been constituted according to a postcolonial logic based on cultural authenticity, the need to address the material effects ensuing from such epistemological assumptions demands an account of how practical human rights mobilization might be envisioned.

It is imperative to avoid insisting on universalizing gay identity, as the basis for rights, and as the only available means of understanding same-sex desire and practice. At least, an interrogative posture is necessary. Why must human rights approaches presuppose an *identitarian telos*? What gains are there on the ground for those people most affected by the crackdowns? How might Egyptian citizens of the underprivileged economic class be better-served through the defense of other human rights, such as freedom of expression and association, privacy, security, freedom from ill-treatment, and torture, etc.? Would not such a defense ensure that a diversity of sexual practices and desires thrive? And is not its protection what defenders of gay rights are ultimately aiming to accomplish anyway? A report issued by Human Rights Watch on the *Queen Boat* case exemplifies an attentive gesture to this end.[70]

Such an interrogative posture ought not to forsake the notion of rights *per se* based on sexual dissidence. If the postcolonial predicament is to be overcome, then a human rights approach that supports and protects sexual dissidents without *necessarily* ascribing an identity to them must equally be contemplated. El Menyawi's proposal based on covert strategies provides a compelling alternative approach that captures a broader notion of rights that includes, but does not *necessarily* presume gay identity. It points to a crucial turning point for future human rights interventions on the ground in the wake of a willfully existent gay subjectivity.

This is especially relevant for local human rights groups and individuals who are confronted with difficult and reductionist choices. The former are caught in a political struggle in which they must decide whether or not to support gay rights, and the latter must reckon with an ontology of *being* homosexual or gay, or not. Indeed, the question of intervention, which articulates the postcolonial predicament, extends to the work of local human rights groups. Egyptian human rights groups had one of two choices: either to support gay rights or oppose them. These human rights groups, in the end, were compelled to "go with the flow" in order to avoid being attacked by the press; going so far as to provide homophobic statements to avoid the accusation of following a Western agenda, to gain popular support, and to send a signal to the Egyptian regime that they are standing by the state against foreign pressures.[71]

Conclusion

Postcolonial critique is necessary to expound on the dynamics of the political struggle. However, *after* the postcolonial state has been incited to constitute gay subjectivity, such critique requires a more nuanced calibration to *strategically* address the reality on the ground where people's lives are at stake. Amr Shalakany elaborates on his discomfort with Massad's critique, contemplating the stakes for local human rights organizations to act in spite of the postcolonial predicament in which they find themselves.[72] The state's urgency in constituting gay subjectivity may well force human rights organizations to take it into account, and ignoring it altogether would not address the state's justification for constituting it in the first place. Although, as Josh Kaplan suggests, human rights interventions overlook the existence of the state of emergency itself, becoming an obstacle to the success of human rights compliance during emergencies: "the focus is nearly always on actions taken, not on the determination of emergency in the first place."[73] This is a crucial point for the success of El Menyawi's proposal. In any case, even if the Gay International might miss the distinction that the problem is in the concept of "gay" as a source of personal and group identification rather than same-sex practices,[74] the state, after being incited to adopt that very epistemology, likewise, *makes* no distinction.[75]

Postcolonial perspectives can still be deployed to inform an understanding of human rights strategies in light of the complexity of the postcolonial condition; for the postcolonial predicament is ultimately relevant for *all* individuals expressing same-sex desire, gay or not. Because state repression will proceed based on Western-based understandings of homosexuality, it will continue to have adverse impacts on those poor and nonurban men in particular, for whom Massad expresses concern, and, who, for better or worse, have been co-opted by both the state and the Gay International within the framework of gay rights discourse. These are the "the poor and nonurban men who practice same-sex contact and who do not identify as homosexual or gay"[76] and who constitute the subaltern in Gayatri Spivak's terms. When epistemic violence has been committed against understandings of local sexual desire, it might be foolish, as Spivak instructs, to presume that there is an ideal subaltern, with an effective voice, who can know and speak itself.[77] Massad's critical dissent—if we are to follow Spivak's argument to its conclusion—does not speak to how the subaltern subject can be separated from the dominant discourse of gay rights and the language and conceptual categories with which it speaks subaltern groups. This is because the subaltern is outside what Spivak calls the "culture of imperialism" and is not intelligible, including to postcolonial natives (or native informants) who are conversant in its language.

The *Queen Boat* case reveals the imperative to constitute the homosexual as a legal subject in order to bring him under Egyptian legal jurisdiction, as both one constituted by the postcolonial state as well as one falling outside its constitution. Inasmuch as international intervention is party to the postcolonial predicament, state violations equally become the plight of those subjects who are brought into the service of nations during times of perceived crisis as others to national identity.[78] How their appeals are to be voiced is the vexing question. It is a question that is intimately tied to the discourse which is derived from the colonial encounter itself, including the discourse of nationalism that saw in decolonization and independence the right to autonomously imitate what Western nations had already achieved.[79]

Human rights interventions need not consider "taking a break from *Orientalism*," a prospect that Amr Shalakany had considered to alleviate the underlying tension between Massad's critique and the urgency for action in the *Queen Boat* case.[80] Sexual rights belong to a structure that one critiques, yet is impossible to dismiss, a structure that one intimately inhabits, as Spivak points out:

> the political claims that are most urgent in decolonized space are tacitly recognized as coded within the legacy of imperialism: nationhood, constitutionality, citizenship, democracy, even culturalism ... what is being *effectively* reclaimed is a series of regulative political concepts, the supposedly authoritative narrative of the production of which was written elsewhere, in the social formations of Western Europe. They are being reclaimed, indeed claimed, as concept-metaphors for which no *historically* adequate referent may be advanced from postcolonial space. That does not make the claims less urgent.[81]

In other words, the critique of gay subjectivity is also "an acknowledgement of the dangerousness of something one cannot not use."[82] For Spivak, the Western provenance of human rights is "in the same category as the 'enabling violation' of the production of the colonial subject."[83] It similarly follows that the production of the gay subject is an enablement that must be used even as the violence of its production is critiqued and renegotiated, because it cannot necessarily be written off in the righting of wrongs.[84] Talal Asad, moreover, adds that European colonial and imperial adventures wrought conditions in which only particular (modern) choices can be made.[85] That the postcolonial subject is "conscripted," involuntarily, to desire progress through modern Western categories that have been inscribed into legal discourse reveals the constraints that condition the modern choices for human rights activism.[86] Resorting to some notion of rights may very well be the most expedient and available way to address the plight of those enduring state oppression. After all, the moorings of gay subjectivity have been anchored well after the boat of critique has sailed.

Notes

[1] These arrests occurred in the wake of the Egyptian government's increased monitoring of the activities of men engaging in homosexual activities on the internet. Subsequent to the establishment of the Internet Crimes Unit at the Interior Ministry, gay chat rooms and matchmaking websites were shut down and several incidents of police entrapment occurred, whereby police arrests were conducted through fake dates from the internet. For a more detailed rendition of the round-up and torture, see Human Rights Watch, *In a Time of Torture: The Assault on Justice in Egypt's Crackdown on Homosexual Conduct*, February 29, 2004, http://www.hrw.org/en/reports/2004/02/29/time-torture (accessed September 4, 2009); Amnesty International, *EGYPT: Torture and Imprisonment for Actual or Perceived Sexual Orientation*, December 19, 2001, http://www.amnesty.org/en/library/info/MDE12/033/2001 (accessed September 4, 2009); and Hossam Bahgat, "Explaining Egypt's Targeting of Gays," *Middle East Report Online*, July 23, 2001, http://www.merip.org/mero/mero072301.html (accessed September 4, 2009).

[2] Bahgat, "Explaining Egypt's Targeting of Gays."

[3] This is an exceptional court created after former President Anwar Sadat was assassinated in 1981; a court which is typically reserved for terrorism and espionage cases. This state of emergency has been continually re-instated by the Egyptian government since the creation of the emergency law and its attendant court. The right of appeal does not extend to the decisions of these courts. Because the office of the current president, Hosni Mubarak, in his capacity as military governor, oversees all cases and appeals in these courts, the independence of the judiciary is effectively eliminated. Because a case could not be made for "contempt of religion," according to one account, it was necessary that a case be found against the detainees because the state had alleged exposing a "specious network." The men were finally charged with the crime of practicing "habitual debauchery" under articles 9 (c) and 15 of Law 10 of 1961 on Combating Prostitution. One man was charged with the crime of "contempt of religion" under article 98 (f) of the Criminal Code and another man for both charges. See Human Rights Watch, *In a Time of Torture*, 41–5 and Amnesty International, *EGYPT: Torture and imprisonment*, 5–8.

[4] Human Rights Watch, *In a Time of Torture*, 45.

[5] Ibid., 46.

[6] Ibid.

[7] Negar Azimi, "Prisoners of Sex," *New York Times Magazine*, December 3, 2006, http://www.nytimes.com/2006/12/03/magazine/03arabs.html (accessed September 4, 2009), 1.

[8] Katherine Franke, "Sexual Tensions of Post-Empire," *Studies in Law, Politics, and Society* 33 (2004): 79.

[9] Ibid., 20–1.

[10] Ibid., 21.

[11] Ibid.

[12] Azimi, "Prisoners of Sex," 1.

[13] Franke, "Sexual Tensions," 21 and Karin van Nieuwkerk, *A Trade Like Any Other: Female Dancers and Singers in Egypt* (Austin, TX: University of Texas Press, 1995), 46–8.

[14] See Nicola Pratt, "The Queen Boat case in Egypt: Sexuality, National Security and State Sovereignty," *Review of International Studies* 33 (2007): 139–40; Philip Smucker, "A Clash of Cultures in Egypt," *The Christian Science Monitor*, September 18, 2001, http://www.csmonitor.com/2001/0918/p6s1-wome.html (accessed September 4, 2009), Azimi, "Prisoners of Sex"; and Scott Long, "The Trials of Culture: Sex and Security in Egypt," *Middle East Report* Online, Spring 2004, http://www.merip.org/mer/mer230/230_long.html (accessed September 4, 2009).

[15] van Nieuwkerk, *A Trade Like Any Other*, 47.
[16] The Capitulations during this period provided legal protection for foreigners in Egypt, and it was "the legal agreement which gave foreigners the right to be tried in their own consular courts. Attempts to bring them to court or to close down their brothels were largely ineffective." van Nieuwkerk, *A Trade Like Any Other*, 45.
[17] Bahgat, "Explaining Egypt's Targeting of Gays," and Human Rights Watch, *In a Time of Torture*, 31.
[18] On the media response to the US legislators' condemnation of the trial, and on the stipulation to resolve outstanding human rights issues in order to ratify the Euro–Mediterranean Association Agreement between Egypt and the European Union, see Human Rights Watch, *In a Time of Torture*, 40 and Amnesty International, *EGYPT*, 8.
[19] Franke, "Sexual Tensions," 22.
[20] Human Rights Watch, *In a Time of Torture*, 7; Bahgat, "Explaining Egypt's Targeting of Gays"; Pratt, "The Queen Boat Case," 134–5; and Hassan El Menywai, "Persecution of Homosexuals: The Egyptian Government's Trojan Horse against Religious Groups," *Human Rights Brief: A Legal Resource for the International Human Rights Community* 14, (2006): 17.
[21] Pratt, "The Queen Boat Case," 135.
[22] Ibid.
[23] Women's rights have relatively benefited in recent years. For example, women were able to finally secure unilateral divorce under Islamic law in 2000 after much resistance. Under the auspices of Egypt's First Lady, the status of women is being raised, reflecting a high level of political commitment to women's initiatives by the presidency, such as campaigns to abolish female genital mutilation.
[24] Pratt, "The Queen Boat Case," 135.
[25] Ibid., 137.
[26] Human Rights Watch, *In a Time of Torture*, 39.
[27] Partha Chatterjee, *The Nation and Its Fragments* (Princeton, NJ: Princeton University Press, 1993), 6.
[28] Ibid.
[29] For an examination of debates on sexuality and how they began to figure in state policy, see Joseph Massad, *Desiring Arabs* (Chicago: University of Chicago Press, 2007), 191–268. In particular, Massad indicates that signs of the inevitability of a crackdown on alleged homosexuals were perceivable, 256.
[30] Human Rights Watch, *In a Time of Torture*, 49.
[31] Giorgio Agamben, *Homo Sacer: Sovereign Power and Bare Life*, trans. Daniel Heller-Roazen (Stanford, CA: Stanford University Press, 1998).
[32] See Human Rights Watch, *In a Time of Torture*, 49 and Azimi, "Prisoners of Sex," 1.
[33] Bahgat, "Explaining Egypt's Targeting of Gays".
[34] Ibid., 18.
[35] Ibid.
[36] See *The Egyptian Constitution*, http://www.egypt.gov.eg/english/laws/constitution (accessed September 4, 2009).
[37] Raymond Williams, *Keywords: A Vocabulary of Culture and Society* (London: Fontana, 1976), 76–82.
[38] Human Rights Watch, *In a Time of Torture*, 14.
[39] See Adel Omar Sherif, "The Rule of Law in Egypt from a Judicial Perspective: A Digest Landmark Decisions of the Supreme Constitutional Court," in *The Rule of Law in the Middle East and the Islamic World: Human Rights and the Judicial Process*, eds. Eugene Cotran and Mai Yamani (London: I.B. Tauris, 2000).

[40] Diane Singerman, "The Politics of Emergency Rule in Egypt," *Current History* 101, (2002): 32.
[41] Hanna Pitkin, "The Idea of a Constitution," *Journal of Legal Education* 37 (1987): 167.
[42] For continued persecution of homosexuals after the *Queen Boat* incident, see Human Rights Watch, *In a Time of Torture*, 49–72 and Amnesty International, *EGYPT*, 14.
[43] Joseph Massad, "Re-orienting Desire: The Gay International and the Arab World," *Public Culture* 14, (2002): 361–85.
[44] Ibid., 362.
[45] Ibid., 363.
[46] Ibid., 364.
[47] Carl Stychin, "The Globalization of Sexual Identities: Universality, Tradition, and the (Post)Colonial Encounter," in *Between Law and Culture: Relocating Legal Studies*, ed. David Theo Goldberg, Michael Musheno, and Lisa C. Bower (Minneapolis: University of Minnesota Press, 2001), 276.
[48] Ibid., 279.
[49] Scholarship on Arab and Muslim desires relied on ahistoricism to render their representations. For further elaboration, see Massad, "Re-orienting Desire," 366.
[50] Stychin, "The Globalization of Sexual Identities," 284.
[51] Brian Whitaker, *Unspeakable Love: Gay and Lesbian Life in the Middle East* (Berkley and Los Angeles: University of California Press, 2006), 11.
[52] For an example of another such context, see Stychin's discussion of the Zimbabwean context, "The Globalization of Sexual Identities," 278.
[53] For elaboration on this point, see Agamben, *Homo Sacer*.
[54] Whitaker, *Unspeakable Love*, 11.
[55] Ibid. (emphasis added).
[56] Ibid., 211–12.
[57] Massad, "Re-orienting Desire," 367.
[58] Whitaker, *Unspeakable Love*, 212.
[59] Whitaker, *Unspeakable Love*, 216.
[60] See Whitaker's discussion on visibility, ibid., 215–16.
[61] Ibid., 216.
[62] Massad, "Re-orienting Desire," 363.
[63] Ibid., 374.
[64] For a detailed discussion of this point, see ibid., 371–85.
[65] Stychin, "The Globalization of Sexual Identities," 281.
[66] Ibid., 281 (emphasis added).
[67] One such example is James Kirchick, "Queer Theory," *The New Republic*, October 15, 2007, http://www.tnr.com/article/politics/queer-theory (accessed September 5, 2009).
[68] Amnesty International, *EGYPT*, 1–2.
[69] Massad specifically mentions the effect of colonialism on Arab and Islamic attitudes towards contraception and the language used to describe sexuality and sexual deviance. See "Re-orienting Desire," 371–2.
[70] Human Rights Watch, *In a Time of Torture*, 1–6. See also Azimi, "Prisoners of Sex," 3 and Amr Shalakany's discussion of the approach adopted by Human Rights Watch in consultation with the *Egyptian Initiative for Personal Rights*, "On a Certain Queer

Discomfort with *Orientalism*," *Proceedings of the American Society of International Law* 101 (2007), http://www.aucegypt.edu/academics/dept/law/faculty/Documents/PROCEEDINGS.pdf (accessed September 4, 2009), 3–4.

[71] Bahgat, "Explaining Egypt's Targeting of Gays." See also Shalakany, "On a Certain Queer Discomfort," 4–5.
[72] See Shalakany, "On a Certain Queer Discomfort."
[73] Josh Kaplan, "The Transnational Human Rights Movement and States of Emergency in Israel/Palestine" in *Deciphering the Global: Its Scales, Spaces and Subjects*, ed. Saskia Sassen (New York: Routledge, 2007), 287.
[74] Massad, "Re-orienting Desire," 382.
[75] Accounts of men interviewed by Human Rights Watch reveal that some men were not invested in, or aware of, gay identity. See Human Rights Watch, *In a Time of Torture*, 4, 10–11.
[76] Massad, "Re-orienting Desire," 384.
[77] Gayatri Chakravorty Spivak, "Can the Subaltern Speak?" in *Marxism and the Interpretation of Culture*, ed. Cary Nelson and Lawrence Grossberg (Chicago: University of Illinois Press, 1988), 271–313.
[78] See Carl F. Stychin, *A Nation by Rights: National Cultures, Sexual Identity Politics and the Discourse of Rights* (Philadelphia, PA: Temple University Press, 1998).
[79] Partha Chatterjee, *Nationalist Thought and the Colonial World: A Derivative Discourse* (Minneapolis, MN: University of Minnesota Press, 1993).
[80] See Shalakany, "On a Certain Queer Discomfort."
[81] Gayatri Chakravorty Spivak, *Outside in the Teaching Machine* (New York: Routledge, 1993), 281 (emphasis in original).
[82] Ibid., 5.
[83] Gayatri Chakravorty Spivak, "Righting Wrongs," in *Human Rights, Human Wrongs: The Oxford Amnesty Lectures 2001*, ed. Nicholas Owen (Oxford: Oxford University Press, 2003), 169.
[84] See ibid.
[85] Talal Asad, "Conscripts of Western Civilization," in *Dialectical Anthropology: Essays in Honor of Stanley Diamond*, ed. Christine Ward Gailey (Gainesville, FL: University Press of Florida, 1992), 337.
[86] Ibid., 340–1.

Index

abduction of children 52–3
abjection, concept of 61
abstraction 18, 35, 42–4
Abu Ghraib 3
action-based approach to human rights 19
action writing 61
activists 1–2, 6, 16, 18, 61–2, 68–70, 73, 99–100, 105–10, 113 *see also* advocacy movements; social movements
advocacy movements 2, 5–6, 17, 46, 48, 61–8, 71–3, 110 *see also* activists; social movements
Aeschylus 89
affirmative rights 44–5
Agamben, Giorgio 102
agency 7, 15, 19, 29–32, 46–8, 50, 53
alternative paradigm of human rights 14–16
Amazon 5–6, 77–92
Amazon Web Services (AWS) 83, 85
anarchy 36, 50–1
androcentricism 12
anonymously, right to read 91
antagonism, human rights as causing 42, 45–6
anthropology 4, 11, 13, 17–22
anti-foundational philosophy 2, 19
anti-globalisation movements 14
aporias of human rights discourse 41–5
articulation 20–1, 53, 57
Asad, Tahal 113
asylum seekers 18, 46, 54 *see also* exiled writers in immigration centres in Australia *see* exiled writers in immigration centres in Australia
authenticity 100–1, 105–10
authoritarianism 53, 67, 105
autonomy 11, 15, 18, 29, 53
autopoiesis 5, 28–30
Awaad, Julian 6

Badiou, Alain 4–5, 47, 48–51, 56
Bakhtin, Mikhail 6, 38, 61, 65
Balibar, Étienne 28–9

Bauman, Zygmunt 51
Baxi, Upendra 14–16, 18
Bechtel Corporation 35
'Before the Law' parable 5, 29–31
Bennett, Tony 12
Berlin, Isaiah 90
Bezos, Jeff 78–83, 89
Bhabha, Homi 6, 62
biopolitics 18
Birkerts, Sven 86
boundaries 20, 52, 86
Brentano, Franz 63
Bruguier, Antoine 89
Butler, Judith 2

capital 12, 16–18, 22–3, 38
capitalism 17–18, 30–1, 34–5, 39, 102
capture and release 34–6
Carr, Nicholas 83
Celan, Paul 64
chance 49
Chatterjee, Partha 101–2
Cheah, Peng 17
child abduction 52–3
choice 17, 21, 44–5, 79
circulations of goods 17
civil and political rights 15
civil rights movement 15, 32, 46
civil society 15, 17, 19
civil war 36
Cochabamba, Peru, water wars of 35
codes and laws 33–4
Cohen, Julie 91
Cold War 16
collective agency 48
collective rights 22
colonialism 6–7, 14, 16, 21, 99–1013
Columbia University Program on Gender, Sexuality, Health and Human Rights 2
commodification of difference 22
communications and development, relationship between 12
communitarianism 51

INDEX

community 2, 11, 20, 55, 102, 107
competition 16, 89–90
constitution of gay subjectivity 99–100, 101–3, 106–7, 110–13
constitutionalism 53–4
constitutions 15, 99, 103–5, 108, 112
contingent, rights as 43
control 5, 18, 29–31, 35, 37, 39, 90
convergence between cultural studies and human rights 3
Coombe, Rosemary 4
cosmopolitanism 12, 17
counterclaims 42, 45
counterpoint 65, 72–3
Cowan, Jane 21
creativity 5–6, 12, 22, 28–9, 34, 36–7, 42, 47, 65
criminal investigations 87–8
critical cultural studies 1–2, 4, 10–23
critical reflexivity 4, 22
critical sociology 2, 19
cultural studies 1–4, 10–23, 43–4
culture: anthropology 20; authenticity 105–9; collective rights 11; critical
cultural studies 1–2, 4, 10–23; critical reflexivity 4, 11; cultural studies 1–4, 10–23, 43–4; dichotomies 4; economic, social or cultural rights 15, 16; Egypt, gay rights in 99, 103–9; exiled writers in immigration centres in Australia 64, 72–4; integrity 11; Kindle 6, 81, 84, 89–91; policy 12; survival 11; trauma 73; wars 16

data mining 5–6, 82–7
de Quincey, Thomas 64
Declaration of the Rights of Indigenous Peoples 15
decolonization 100–2, 112
deconstructionism 3, 10, 14, 16–17, 67–8
definition of law 29
dehumanization 67–8
Deleuze, Gilles 30–2, 34, 49
democracy 15, 17, 37, 50–1
Denmark, conflict resolution in 54–7: affect and libidinal conflicts 5, 54, 56; Christian Democrats 54–5; ethics, ideology of 56–7; forced marriages 54; *gacacas* in Rwanda 55; gatherings 54–5; immanence 56–7; mediation 54–6; mosques, construction of 54; Muslims 54–6; narratives of Truth 56–7; polygamy 55; Social Democrats 54–5; witnessing 56–7
dependency 50
Derrida, Jacques 5, 31
detention 3 *see also* exiled writers in immigration centres in Australia
deterritorialization 53

détournment 90
development 1, 12, 22
deviancy 67–8
dialectics 3
dialogism 65, 72–3
dichotomies 4, 12
difference 15, 22, 48
disassociation 64
discipline 11, 17, 37, 39
discourse theory 10, 13–18, 20, 29, 44–5
dispute resolution 3, 30, 32, 42–6, 53–7
dissidence 52, 109–11
diversity 11, 14, 16, 22, 38, 62, 110–11
divine law 33
domestic violence after separation 52–4
dominant bodies 48–9
Donnelly, Jack 1
double counterpoint 65, 72–3
Douzinas, Costas 13–14, 16, 18, 20

economic, social or cultural rights 15, 16
education 11, 32, 103
Egypt, gay rights in 6, 98–113: activists 99–100, 105–10; authenticity 100–1, 105–10; Constitution 99, 103–5, 108, 112; constitution of gay subjectivity 99–100, 101–3, 106–7, 110–13; culture 99, 103–9; decolonization 100–2, 112; distraction, policy of 103; economic crisis 101–3; emergency laws 99, 104–5, 111; epistemology of gay rights 105–11; 'Gay International' 99, 105–12; gender norms 101, 103; globalization 99, 101–2, 106; heteronormativity 101; identity 102, 105–6, 108–10; incitement 109–10; intervention by international human rights organizations 99, 105–7, 109–12; Islam 98–105, 107, 110; media 99; modernity 101, 105; Muslim Brotherhood 101, 102–3; national security 104; nationalism 6, 101–2, 106–8, 112; neoliberal globalization 99, 101–2; ontology 111; Orientalism 6, 106–7, 112; post-colonialism 6–7, 99–107, 109–13; prostitution, foreign colonialism and 100, 102; *Queen Boat 52* case 6–7, 98–106, 109–12; religion 6, 99, 101–5, 107, 110; sexual dissidence 109–11; sexuality and decolonization 100–1; state sovereignty 100–2, 105, 107; subaltern studies 7, 112; subjectivity 99–100, 101–3, 106–7, 110–13; torture 98–9; universalism 6, 99, 105, 108, 110; values and norms 101, 103–4; visibility 108–9; West 6, 99, 102, 105–9, 111–13

INDEX

empiricism 5, 19
Enlightenment 14–15, 21
environment 11, 23
epistemology 4, 67, 105–11
essentialism 14, 20, 33
ethics 5, 18–19, 48–50, 56–7
ethnicity 14, 53–4, 62
ethnography 4, 11, 13, 21
Eurocentricism 12
events 33–5, 57
evil 5, 47, 49–50, 56
exclusion 12–13, 14
exiled writers in immigration centres in Australia 6, 61–74: advocacy movements 61–2, 66–8, 71–3; Australian Human Rights Commission 61, 65–6, 68, 71–2; changing policies 71–2; charges for detention 72; counterpoint 65, 72–3; culture 64, 72–4; dehumanization and deviancy, deconstruction of 67–8; dialogism 65, 72–3; double counterpoint 65, 72–3; episteme of postindustrial late modernity 67; fugal critical analysis 61–3, 72–3; fugal modality 64–5; fugal recursion 65, 72; fugal reflection 73–4; fugal writing 6, 64–5, 72–3; fugue 6, 61–5, 69, 72–4; international human rights law 65–7; Iranian poet-musician, arbitrary detention in Australia of 6, 61–2, 66, 67–70; Ivory Coast journalist, arbitrary detention in Australia of 6, 61–2, 67, 70–3; limbo, state of 66; media representation of refugees 61, 67–8, 73; memory involuntary 65, 73; metaphor, as 6, 63–4; modal shift from reading about to writing of 6, 61, 63–4; musical counterpoint 61–2; negative stereotyping 68; non-governmental organisations 61; Pacific Solution 61–2, 65–6, 71–2; PEN (Poets, Essayists, Novelists) 61–2, 67–8, 70–2; phenomenological experience 6, 63–4, 72; polyphony 61, 65, 72; reflexive practices 6, 61, 64, 73; research 62–4, 72; Tampa Incident 66; Temporary Protection Visas 61–2, 66, 71–2; trauma 64, 66–7, 68–70, 72–4; Writers in Detention Committee 62, 68; zone of indeterminacy 67; zones of excision 65–6
expression, freedom of 61, 74, 86, 91

Fanon, Franz 2
Feldman, Allen 3
feminism 2, 3, 63, 100
forced marriages 54
Foucault, Michel 2, 5, 17, 35, 61, 67, 73, 109
foundationalism 2, 19, 33, 47–8, 51, 54
free labour 84, 86
freedom 17–18, 28–9, 37, 47–8
freedom of expression 61, 74, 86, 91
Freud, Sigmund 73
fugal critical analysis 61–3, 72–3
fugal modality 64–5
fugal writing 6, 63–5, 72–3
fugue 6, 61–5, 69, 72–4
Fundamentalist Latter Day Saints (FLDS) 55

gacacas in Rwanda 55
Gandy, Oscar 84
gates and gatekeepers 5, 29–31
Gawronski, Justin D 88–9
'Gay International' 99, 105–12
gay rights *see* Egypt, gay rights in
gender 2, 101, 103 *see also* feminism
Genette, Gerard 80
Geneva Conventions 46
geopolitics 18
gesetz (law) and *recht* (justice) 29
ghost in the machine 30–1
gift from the West, human rights as a 14
Giroux, Henry 3
global and the local 51–4
globalization 14, 16–17, 19, 22, 36, 38, 99, 101–2, 106
God 29, 35, 37–8
good 49–50, 56
Goodale, Mark 20
goodwill 84, 89
governance 3, 14, 16–18, 37, 45, 50, 53
government technologies 5, 17
governmentality 5, 11, 13, 17, 18, 22
Gramsci, Antonio 2
Grewal, Inderpal 17
group identity 19–20
Guattari, Felix 32
Gutmann, Amy 47

Habermas, Jürgen 1, 45
Hall, Gary 81
Halley, Janet 1
Hardt, Michael 28, 29, 36–8
Hawes, Leonard 4–5
health 2, 18, 36, 55–6, 66, 70
hegemony 1, 13–18, 22, 47, 67
Herderian Romantic nationalism 11
heritage, collective rights to cultural 11
hermeneutics 10, 21
heteroglossia 38
heteronormativity 101
heterosexism 12, 101
hierarchy 15, 20, 38
Hobbes, Thomas 36–7
homosexuality *see* Egypt, gay rights in
hostage-taking 54
human rights markets 16–17
humanitarianism as an industry 18
humanity 17, 47–8, 50, 68, 89

INDEX

identity 4, 12–15, 19–22, 102, 105–6, 108–10
Ignatieff, Michael 4, 42, 46–7, 50–2
imaginaries 3–4, 7, 12, 14–15, 19–21, 51
immanence 5, 27–39, 43–4, 49–51, 56–7
imminence 4–5
immortal 48, 50
incitement 109–10
inclusion 12–13, 62
independence and solidarity 44–5
indeterminacy of rights 4, 42, 44
indigenous people 15, 23
inequality 4, 17–18, 50
information 12, 83, 84, 87–8
information technology 12
informational capital 12
ingesting the state, act of 35
instability of rights 4, 42, 44–5, 53, 101
instantiation 33, 35, 38
institutions 2, 3, 7, 17, 19, 54
intellectual property 12
intentionality, modality of 63
interdisciplinary work 2, 22
international law 1, 3, 14, 65–7
International Monetary Fund (IMF) 16
interpellation 19, 23
interpretive practice 2, 19
intervention 99, 105–7, 109–12
iPad 78–9, 81
Iranian poet-musician, arbitrary detention in Australia of 6, 61–2, 66,67–70
Islam/Muslims 54–6, 98–105, 107, 110
Ivory Coast journalist, arbitrary detention in Australia of 6, 61–2, 67, 70–3

Johnson, Richard 12
Joyce, James 64
juridical and immanent law 27–39
jurisprudence 33
just (natural order) 29
justice 14, 19, 21, 29, 50–1

Kafka's 'Before the Law' parable 5, 29–31
Kandinsky, Vasily 69
Kantian philosophy 2
Kaplan, Josh 111
Keating, Paul 72
Keneally, Thomas 62, 68
Kennedy, David 18
Kindle 5–6, 77–92; Amazon 5–6, 77–92; Amazon Web Services (AWS) 83, 85; anonymously, right to read 91; competition 89–90; criminal investigations 87–8; culture 6, 81, 84, 89–91; data mining 5–6, 82–7; deactivation of accounts 78; *détournment* 90; downstream capabilities 81–2; free labour 84, 86; freedom of expression 86, 91; goodwill 84, 89; human intelligence tasks 85; illiberal object, as 5–6, 79; liberal politics 79, 90–1; liberal propriety 5–6, 90; literacy 5–6, 79, 90–2; Mechanical Turk website 85; paradox of the e-book 79–82; paratechnology 80; paratextuality 80; personal information 83, 84, 87–8; privacy 86–8; property rights, fruits of reading as 84–5; propriety of reading 84–8; reading labour 5, 84, 86; reading, rights of 5–6, 91; searches and seizures 87–8; simulating and exceeding books, as 5, 80–2; sovereignty of readers 6, 86, 88; surplus value, capture of 5–6; surveillance 6, 86–8; tethered appliances 78, 82, 86–7, 89–91; value 84–5; Whispersync 82
knowledge 17–18, 23
Kone, Cheikh 6, 61–2, 67, 70–3
Kristeva, Julia 6, 61, 64
Kurasawa, Fuyuki 19
Kymlicka, Will 2

labour disputes 3
Langlois, Anthony J 32
language 19–20, 29, 38, 54–5, 64–5, 73, 82, 108–10
law, definition of 29
legal anthropology 4, 19–20
legal cultural studies 3–7
legal positivism 32–3
less developed countries, intervention in 18
Lessig, Lawrence 91
lex (state-mandated order) and *just* (natural order) 29
liberalism 5–6, 14–15, 51, 79, 90–1
liberative capacity 5, 28
libidinal conflicts 5, 54, 56
literacy 5–6, 79, 90–2
local practices 18–22
Luhmann, Niklas 29

MacIntyre, Alasdair 51
majority rights 53
managing populations 18
Manguel, Alberto 79, 86
markets 16–17
Marr, David 68
Marx, Karl 2, 3, 36, 86
Massad, Joseph 99, 105–12
measurement of values 44
Mechanical Turk website 85
media 15, 16, 61, 67–8, 73, 99
mediation 30, 32, 43–6, 54–6
Mercer, Colin 12
military policy-making 18
Mill, John Stuart 86
Miller, Toby 3, 19

INDEX

mind, law of nature implanted in the human 29–30
Mindell, Arnold 48
minorities 6, 11, 53
modernity 101, 105
Mohsen 6, 61–2, 66, 67–70
morality 5, 18–19, 48–50, 56–7
Morson, Gary Saul 34
Mubarak, Hosni 99, 102–3
multiculturalism 3, 12, 14
multinationals 16
multitude 5, 28, 36–9
musical counterpoint 61–2
Muslim Brotherhood 101, 102–3
Muslims/Islam 54–6, 98–105, 107, 110

Nabokov, Vladimir 86
narratives 56–7
nation states, stability of 51–3
national security 104
nationalism 3, 6, 11, 14, 17, 48, 101–2, 106–8, 112
natural law 2, 29–30, 33
natural order *(just)* 29
natural rights 37
needs as rights 43
negative freedoms 47
negative rights 44–5, 48, 50, 52
negative stereotyping 68
Negri, Antonio 28, 29, 36–8
neoliberalism 1, 13–18, 20, 22–3, 99, 101–2
networks 5, 17, 19, 36, 91–2, 102
Nietzsche, Friedrich 49
Nolan, Sydney 69–70
non-evil, human rights are rights to 49
non-governmental organisations (NGOs) 15, 17–18, 61
norms 15–16, 33, 99, 101, 103–4, 106
Nussbaum, Martha 1

One and the Same 49
Ong, Walter 81–2
ontology 4–5, 31–3, 39, 48–51, 111
oppositional critique of law 2, 45–8, 52
oppression 14, 17–18, 42, 46–7, 50, 105, 113
Orford, Anne 18
Orientalism 6, 106–7, 112
Orwell, George 88–9
Other, ethical ideology of the 48–50

Pacific Solution 61–2, 65–6, 71–2
paratechnology 80
paratextuality 80
particularism/universalism 12
patriarch 54
pedagogy 3, 17–18

PEN (Poets, Essayists, Novelists) 61–2, 67–8, 70–2
people, notion of the 36
personal information, Kindle and 83, 84, 87–8
personal relationships 51–4
phenomenological experience 6, 63–4, 72
photographs, pedagogical potential of 3
Pickering, Sharon 67
Plath, Sylvia 64
pluralism 14, 47, 54
politics 3–7, 11–19, 22, 37–8, 44–5, 49, 51, 79, 90–1
polygamy 55
polyphony 61, 65, 72
poor 1, 18, 101, 108
population welfare, indices of 17
positive law 2
positive rights 44–5, 48, 52
positivism 32–3
post-colonialism 6–7, 99–107, 109–13
post-modernism 2, 30–1
post-structuralism 14, 19
potentialities 45–6, 57
power 1, 3–4, 13, 17, 23
practices 2, 11–12, 18–23
practitioners, social capital of rights 17
privacy 86–8
privilege 48–9
probability theory 49
productive acts 35–6
professional humanitarians 18
progressive social forces, rights as impeding 42–3
prostitution 100, 102
Proust, Marcel 64
psychiatry, refusal 36
psychoanalysis 3, 11, 14

Queen Boat 52 case 6–7, 98–106, 109–12

racism 14, 62
radical contingency of human rights 15
Rajagopal, Balakrishnan 1, 14–15
rationality/reason 14, 29, 51, 107
reactive rights 44–5
reading 5–6, 84–8, 91
rebellion 13–14
recht (justice) 29
recognition justice 68
recognition 3, 14, 23, 35, 43, 47–8, 52–3, 62, 68
reductionism 2–3, 32, 81, 111
reflexive practices 6, 61, 64, 73
refugees 18, 46, 54 *see also* exiled writers in immigration centres in Australia

INDEX

regional charters 15
registers of law 29–32
reification 12, 42, 44
relativism 4, 12, 21
release, capture and 34–6
religion 6, 54–6, 98–105, 107, 110
rescuers 50
research 12, 62–4, 72
resistance 13–14, 62
rhetoric 10, 12–13, 15, 22, 41
Rorty, Richard 51
Rose, Charlie 77–80
Ross, Andrew 3
Rudd, Kevin 71–2
rule of conduct imposed by authority 29–30, 31–2
rule of law 50–1
ruleship 18
rural economic revitalization 22
Rwanda, *gacacas* in 55

Said, Edward W 61, 62
sameness 4, 15, 21, 48–9, 57
Santos, Boaventura de Sousa 1
scarcity conditions 50
Schumpeter, Joseph 42
science and technology studies 10
Scott, Rosie 62, 66, 68
searches and seizures 87–8
secession 52–3
security 50–1
selective tolerance of difference 48
self-determination 48, 50–4
semiotics 10, 14
Sen, Armatya 1
separation, domestic violence after 52–3
servitude 54
sexuality 2, 5 *see also* Egypt, gay rights in
Shalakany, Amr 111–12
Sha'rawi, Huda 100
Skilbeck, Ruth 5
Skott-Myhre, Hans 4–5
slavery 46
social capital 17, 23
social communities, practice of 12
social consciousness 7
social context 64
social forces, rights as impeding progressive 42–3
social hierarchies 15, 20
social identity 19
social imaginary structures 7
social inclusion 62
social justice 14
social movements 1–2, 14–15, 17, 22, 32, 46
  see also activists; advocacy movements
social positions, rights as fixing 4
social production of rights 38
social rights 15, 16

social subjectivity 37–8
socialist countries, intervention in former 18
sociocultural context of rights violations 43–4
socio-legal theory 1–2
sociology 2, 17
solidarity 44–5
solidification of position 42
Solove, Daniel J 87
sovereign discipline 37
sovereignty of readers 6, 86, 88
specific rights, recognition of invocation of 43–4
Spinoza, Baruch 5, 29, 31, 36–7
Spivak, Gayatri 112–13
state sovereignty 5, 28–9, 32–9, 48, 100–12, 105, 107
Striphas, Ted 5
Stychin, Carl 106, 109
subaltern studies 2, 7, 15, 112
subject as *subjectus* 28–9, 31–4
subject formation 5, 11, 17–19
subjectivity 23, 37–8, 99–100, 101–3, 106–7, 110–13
subnational cultural rights 11
subordination of victims 48–9
suffering 45
superior, humans as 43
supplicants 5, 29–31
surveillance 6, 86–8
sustainable livelihoods 22

Tampa Incident 66
Tarulli, Donato 4–5
Temporary Protection Visas 61–2, 66, 71–2
territory 15, 34, 53
terrorism 52
tethered appliances 78, 82, 86–7, 89–91
'Throw of the Dice' figure 49
tolerance of differences 48
torture 3, 52, 98–9
traditions 19–20, 22
transcendence 5, 17, 30, 33, 41–50
transnationalism 11, 17–18, 22
trauma 64, 66–7, 68–70, 72–4
trumps, rights as 13, 41–2
truth 5, 41–50, 56–7
Turner, Bryan 1
Tushnet, Mark 42, 44–5

United Nations (UN) 2, 14, 65
United States 3, 15–18, 32, 46, 55
Universal Declaration of Human Rights 46
universality 4–6, 11–12, 17, 20–1, 33, 43–52, 56, 99, 104, 108, 110

values 44, 50–1, 101, 103–4
Vance, Carol 2
vernacularization 21–2
Viereck, Rosa 69

INDEX

victims 42, 45, 48–50
Virno, Paolo 36

Walzer, Michael 51
Waters, Malcolm 2
West 6, 14, 44–5, 99, 102, 105–9, 111–13
which-is-not-yet position 4–5, 49
Whitaker, Brian 106–8
Whispersync 82
white nationalism 17
Williams, Patricia 1
Williams, Raymond 79

Winfrey, Oprah 77–8, 91–2
witnessing 19, 56–7
word and world, relationship between 12
World Bank 17, 18
World Social Forum (WSF) 1
World Trade Organization (WTO) 16
writers *see* exiled writers in immigration centres in Australia

Yudice, George 4, 13, 22

Zittrain, Jonathan 78

9781138008953